VIRTUAL POWER

VIRTUAL POWER

THE FUTURE OF ENERGY FLEXIBILITY

WILLIAM ANGEL

NEW DEGREE PRESS

COPYRIGHT © 2020 WILLIAM ANGEL

All rights reserved.

VIRTUAL POWER

The Future of Energy Flexibility

ISBN   978-1-64137-423-1   *Paperback*

            978-1-64137-424-8   *Kindle Ebook*

            978-1-64137-425-5   *Digital Ebook*

To my parents, Jim and Amy

CONTENTS

ACKNOWLEDGMENTS

——

I would like to thank Brien Bies and Eric Koester for convincing me to write this book, and all the staff and contributing editors at New Degree Press, including Jonathan Jordan, Cynthia Tucker, Lyn Solares, Gjorgji Pejkovski, Leila Summers, Amanda Brown, Tracy Seybold, and everyone else working behind the scenes to make this book happen. This would not have been possible without you all. Likewise, I am deeply grateful for all the other authors publishing with New Degree Press for their motivation and comradery.

My sincere thanks to all the people who have been gracious with their time and let me rant and rave about the electrical grid and virtual power plants, including but not limited to Kyle Smitz, Hugh Youngblood, Adam Irwin, Mihaela Ulieru, Alex Mitchell, Jeff Rodgers, and many others.

I have great gratitude for everyone who supported this book, including JJ Wanda, Adam Jacobson, Ying Wang, Tom Hine, Alex Bayani, Cristina Ibarra, Lorraine Slattery, Karen Skelton, Marilyn Ichioka, Victor Ichioka, Brian Lint, Patrick Soltis, June Phang, Stephen Foster, Katie Hyland, Andrew

Chester, Joy Hughes, Adam Pijanowski, Andrew Gutman, Ian Burns, Isaac Shomer, Hector Garrido, Christine Millett, Elizabeth Biener, Maura Lint, James Angel, Amy Angel, Elizabeth Angel, Alyssa Lovegrove, Nick Lovegrove, Gabriel Gorre, Rolando Pena, Will Skelton, Jeff Jale, Greg Phillips, Young Chang, Jennifer Duggins, Oscar Merrit-Nestell, Erica El-Hady, Manjia Gong, Casey Knerr, Jay Knerr, Richard Poundstone, Joan Poundstone, Masha Stoianova, Anson Rutherford, John Angel, Karen Kinard, Tom Lint, Celeste Land, Mayze Teitler, David Frye, Justin Michaud, and those who wished to remain pseudonymous including Theemosunrise, Liz_en, and my dear friend Ligma B. A'lze.

To everyone I have omitted due to error, negligence, or procrastination, thank you.

And of course, to my darling Margo, who said that I should write a blog first.

INTRODUCTION

Mother's Day, May 8, 2016, was a beautiful spring day in Germany. The sun was shining; the wind was blowing; wind, solar, hydro, and other renewable energy sources were generating almost 87 percent of the electricity produced in the country…and the wholesale price of electricity was negative from 7:00 a.m. to 5:00 p.m., reaching a low of -130 euros per megawatt-hour at 1:00 p.m.[1] German utilities spent millions of euros paying people to consume excess electricity, on top of the 200 billion euros that had been spent to date on renewable generation.

Free electricity may sound appealing, but pricing anomalies like this actually increase the overall cost of the system and result in increased carbon emissions. This same story is being told around the world: wind and solar electrical generation are being installed on a local, national, and planetary-scale and are causing increases in costs, carbon emissions, and

---

1   Michael J. Coren, "Germany Had so Much Renewable Energy on Sunday That It Had to Pay People to Use Electricity," Quartz (Quartz, May 11, 2016), https://qz.com/680661/germany-had-so-much-renewable-energy-on-sunday-that-it-had-to-pay-people-to-use-electricity/).

blackouts. More renewable energy can increase the operating costs and carbon emissions of an electrical network. This paradox is one of the largest challenges facing attempts to decarbonize energy.

RENEWABLES ARE TOO CHEAP TO IGNORE
The cost of renewables has come down so much that wind and solar are usually cheaper than new coal and gas generation, sometimes costing less than half as much per generated megawatt over a resource's lifetime. In some extreme cases, building new solar installations is cheaper than the marginal cost of continuing to run an existing coal plant!

This trend of falling costs is projected to continue over the next ten to thirty years. Cheaper low-carbon renewable resources will be an essential component for meeting the ambitious carbon emission goals laid out in the 2015 Paris Climate Conference, as these lower costs are resulting in a faster adoption of renewable energy. The speed at which this is happening makes the flexibility issue an urgent problem for utilities and grid operators.

Serendipitously, the cost of energy storage is falling as rapidly as solar panels did a decade ago. These cost decreases, while miraculously timed, are the result of hard work and massive investments in research, development, and commercialization by corporations, governments, and brilliant scientists across the planet. Predictions suggest that the cost of many energy storage technologies will fall by 50 to 60 percent or more by 2030. Cost reductions will create more opportunities for projects and investments in storage technology, which will help decrease the cost of storage even faster as the technology and businesses mature.

Predictions on the cost of wind and solar over the last ten to twenty years—even some of the most aggressive and optimistic predictions—have turned out to be wrong. Wind and solar have decreased in cost faster than most industry experts predicted. This surprisingly fast fall in prices is mostly attributable to the learning curve for solar: as companies made more solar cells and panels, they got better. The cost decreases in storage may follow this same trend, which would result in even faster adoption and results. Trillions of dollars of existing energy assets could be rendered unprofitable by 2050 if the cost of storage and renewables continues to fall at expected rates, potentially sooner if the costs fall faster than predicted.

THE PARADOX OF RENEWABLE ENERGY

This book will explore the paradoxical result that the greater adoption of renewable energy resources can cause and expose the inflexibility of electrical networks to integrate zero-emission variable sources of energy. This investigation will include an overview of the technological developments, economic forces, and regulatory headaches shaping the electrical grid of the twenty-first century and provide a look into the global efforts to decarbonize electrical generation.

If you are interested in the technology, economics, or government policy related to energy, this book will provide you with an in-depth look at how energy storage and flexible generation and demand are going to be critical to modernize the electrical grid over the next thirty years and beyond. If you are someone who is passionate about the environment and sustainability, anxious about blackouts and lines at gas stations, and interested in the future, this book was written for you. If you aren't, maybe this book will convince you that you should become someone like that; someone who is invested in renewable energy and a healthy planet.

Here are some of the most important concepts that you will take away from this book:

- How we can generate, store, and consume electricity with minimum environmental pollution
- Insights into how the next ten years will improve energy security and make the grid more reliable and resilient
- A look into how energy storage will help save the planet and radically reshape the energy landscape
- How virtual power plants and networked distributed energy resources will increase the grid's flexibility

GRID FLEXIBILITY AND DEMOCRATIZATION

The deployment of large quantities of variable generation—wind and solar that cannot be dispatched like conventional generation whenever a utility needs it—and their rising market penetration is making it obvious that our electrical grids are insufficiently flexible to accommodate democratization. Market deregulation over the last twenty to thirty years combined with the rapid cost decreases in renewables means that individual consumers, communities, and businesses have unprecedented ability to choose where their energy comes from and profit off any extra electricity they generate. This democratization of electrical generation has caught many utilities by surprise, causing prices to rise to cover the grid operators' lack of preparations. This scissor effect of rising grid prices and decreasing costs for renewables and off-grid generation is causing this transition from centralized generation to distributed generation to accelerate.

Despite the increasing speed of this transition, we are still in the early stages and have a long way to go. The US Energy Information Agency's short-term energy outlook for October 2019 has the United States on track to generate 10 percent of total electrical production—414 billion kilowatt-hours—from non-hydro renewable sources. Some US states have committed to generating 100 percent of their electricity from zero-carbon emission sources by 2045 or 2050. The next thirty years will be pivotal as the world transitions further from fossil fuels toward low-carbon energy sources, from centralized generation to more distributed generation resources, and from "dumb" loads to smarter and more responsive demand.

Energy storage and virtual power plant technologies provide the flexibility needed to move toward a sustainable low-carbon future. I believe that distributed energy storage and virtual power plants made of distributed energy resources are the fastest and lowest-cost ways to integrate variable energy resources into the electrical network. If implemented correctly within a good regulatory environment, these technologies will reduce costs and carbon emissions while increasing grid resiliency and reliability in the face of increasingly adverse environmental conditions.

1

THE CHALLENGE

———

Saving our planet, lifting people out of poverty, advancing economic growth…these are one and the same fight. We must connect the dots between climate change, water scarcity, energy shortages, global health, food security, and women's empowerment. Solutions to one problem must be solutions for all.
—BAN KI-MOON, ADDRESS TO THE 66TH GENERAL ASSEMBLY

CLIMATE CHANGE

We face a challenge of planetary and existential proportions. Human activities are causing changes to the global biosphere and climate, which in turn have detrimental effects on human and animal life. These negative impacts and changes are projected to become more severe for most regions over the remainder of the century.

In some areas, such as parts of Canada and Russia, a warmer climate may have slight positive benefits. Other areas will suffer apocalyptic environmental changes if major corrective actions are not taken immediately.

Take my hometown of Washington, DC, as an example: climate models indicate that by the year 2100, Washington, DC, will experience a 300 to 900 percent increase in days above ninety-five degrees Fahrenheit and one to three meters of sea-level rise.[2] The lower end of these projections is likely in a scenario where global warming is limited to an increase of two degrees Celsius—which is currently considered to be a reachable but ambitious and optimistic goal. The upper end of these projections can be expected with four degrees of warming. Four degrees of warming is well below a "business as usual" future scenario where energy consumption does not change any faster.

Our changing climate is caused primarily by human activities. The biggest driver of climate change is global heating caused by the increasing amount of greenhouse gases in our atmosphere. This increase is driven primarily by increased emissions of greenhouse gases from human activities, mostly from carbon dioxide emitted for transportation, industrial uses, and electrical generation.

There is also a decrease in the amount of carbon consumed by global biomass: in other words, deforestation is reducing the number of plants that are responsible for converting carbon dioxide to oxygen.

Of the human sources of greenhouse gas emissions, close to 75 percent of total greenhouse gas emissions are emitted by

2   "FUTURE: Rising Temperatures and Floods in Washington, DC," Tipping Points: Global Climate Change, Made Local, accessed January 12, 2020, https://www.climatetippingpoints.com/places/washington-dc-future-climate-change).

the twenty largest countries.[3] Of these emissions, 93 percent come from energy and industry (counting agricultural emissions as industry). Nearly three-quarters of these emissions come from industry and energy consumption. In the United States, about 73 percent of greenhouse gas emissions come from energy use, including:

- Electrical power generation—33 percent
- Consumption of gasoline, diesel, and nonaviation transportation fuels—30 percent

This means that more than 60 percent—almost two-thirds—of total carbon emissions in the United States are emitted in transportation and electricity generation.[4]

With vehicle electrification and zero emissions renewable energy technology, it appears that we have the technology to reduce planetary carbon emissions to near zero.

Solar panels have been used commercially since the 1960s, and electric cars were invented before the internal combustion engine—indeed, in the year 1900, there were more electric cars than gasoline cars in the United States[5]—so why is the world currently dependent on fossil fuels?

---

3 Hal Harvey, Robbie Orvis, Jeffrey Rissman. *Designing Climate Solutions.*

4 Monthly Energy Review, US Energy Information Administration, 2019, https://www.eia.gov/totalenergy/data/monthly/index.php#environment.

5 "The History of the Electric Car," US Department of Energy. Energy. gov, accessed January 12, 2020, https://www.energy.gov/articles/history-electric-car.

The answers are cost and reliability. Along with sustainability, cost and reliable access make up The Energy Trilemma.

THE ENERGY TRILEMMA

Energy policy is hard because of the trilemma between three objectives that usually are mutually incompatible: security, affordability, and sustainability.

These three objectives are critical for the consumption of most energy and can be easily observed in the questions people ask about energy:

- "How do I get it?"
- "How much does it cost?"
- "Is it safe?"

Different people, businesses, and governments make these trade-offs daily when deciding what energy-producing and -consuming equipment they'll invest in and how to use it.

SECURITY

The first point of the trilemma, energy security, is usually the most important concern of policymakers at the global, national, regional, and personal level. Secure access to a constant supply of energy is critical to civilization. Without constant access to energy, modern civilization stops working, and people die due to disruption of service, lack of supply chains, and loss of life-support systems. While a total loss of all forms of energy is impossible—the wind will always be blowing for wind energy, the sun shining for solar and thermal, and trees and plants growing for biomass and bio-fuels—major disruptions in the form of shortages and price increases are a serious risk.

Current geopolitical conflicts are driven by energy and access to energy. More than 30 percent of all the crude oil shipped through maritime routes in 2016 transited through the South China Sea.[6] China's nautical territory claims extend into international waters and cover most of the South China Sea. Nearly 90 percent of the crude oil Japan and South Korea imported in 2016 passed through the South China Sea, which means that the bulk of their oil consumption is dependent on open navigation through waters that China increasingly is asserting influence and military control over.

The Strait of Hormuz is another geopolitical flashpoint caused by access to energy. This waterway between Oman, the United Arab Emirates, and Iran is a major artery for the global oil industry. Iranian oil exports are currently sanctioned by the United Nations, and Iran is being accused of sabotaging several tankers with explosive mines in an attempt to reduce the oil exports of Saudi Arabia and other oil exporters that benefit from Iranian oil never making it to work markets.[7] Before the 2012 sanctions went into place, Iran was bringing in approximately $100 billion in

---

6   More than 30 percent of global maritime crude oil trade moves through the South China Sea—Today in Energy—US Energy Information Administration (EIA), accessed January 12, 2020, https://www.eia.gov/todayinenergy/detail.php?id=36952.

7   Jon Gambrell, The Associated Press. "Tankers Struck Near Strait of Hormuz; US Blames Iran," June 13, 2019, https://apnews.com/d67714ab8ac344a3b3af19cca1c20192.

oil exports—more than half of their annual budget. Iran's threats to close the strait created anxiety that the flow of oil from the Middle East could be radically reduced. This threat led to nearly record prices in 2012 in an echo of the mining of the Strait of Hormuz during the Iran-Iraq war in the early 1980s. The US Energy Information Agency considers the Strait of Hormuz to be the most important chokepoint for the oil industry: in 2018, 21 percent of global oil consumption flowed through the strait daily.[8]

Access to energy, specifically oil, has driven American foreign policy explicitly for forty years since the Carter doctrine declared that an attack on the Persian Gulf was an attack on American interests. In President Carter's State of the Union Speech in January of 1980, he addressed the recent Soviet invasion of Afghanistan and the revolution in Iran:

"Let our position be absolutely clear: An attempt by any outside force to gain control of the Persian Gulf region will be regarded as an assault on the vital interests of the United States of America, and such an assault will be repelled by any means necessary, including military force."[9]

Overall, the security of an energy source and how reliable access is expected to be are large factors in evaluating energy

---

8   "The Strait of Hormuz is the world's most important oil transit chokepoint—Today in Energy—US Energy Information Administration (EIA), accessed January 12, 2020, https://www.eia.gov/todayinenergy/detail.php?id=39932.

9   "January 23, 1980: State of the Union Address," Miller Center, May 3, 2017, https://millercenter.org/the-presidency/presidential-speeches/january-23-1980-state-union-address.

resources. Rhetoric around the virtues of self-reliance or condemning the dangerous reliance on foreign energy supplies is commonplace in political debates around this subject.

AFFORDABILITY

The second point of the Energy Trilemma is affordability. Access to energy must be affordable and widespread. Equitable economic growth is contingent on access to electricity and energy. To improve the quality of life and standards of living on a planetary scale, more energy is required. Almost 13 percent of humans alive today do not have reliable access to electricity, and 40 percent lack access to clean cooking fuels.

One in eight people currently lacks access to electricity. The World Bank started tracking and collecting data about the percentage of national populations that have access to electricity in 1990. At the time, 71 percent of the global population had access to electricity. At last count in 2016, this number had increased to 87 percent.

This 16 percent increase in access to electricity happened despite the world population increasing by 41 percent from 5.29 billion in 1990 to 7.44 billion in 2016. Through demographic changes and development, much of this population growth has accrued in cities where the electrification rate is high.

The global percentage of urban residents with access to electricity reached 97 percent in 2016. Globally, electrical access in rural areas was 77 percent at the time of this writing.[10]

The economic miracle of the last thirty years has been remarkable. More people today have electricity than were alive in 1990. We have globally increased access to electricity and more importantly, many of the benefits that come with electricity, like cheaper and cleaner cooking and lighting, by more than two and a half billion people from 1990 to 2016. This is a great accomplishment, especially with how critical electricity is for modern telecommunications and the increasingly digital nature of economic access.

However, this means that almost one billion people still lack electricity. Many, though not all, of these people are some of the world's poorest and most disadvantaged. The economic growth that will come from further integrating these people into the global economy will be massive. The world economy doubled in absolute value from 1993 to 2017, growing from $39 trillion (2010 USD) to $81 trillion, largely because of China.

China's economy increased in size from $1.1 trillion to $10.2 trillion, accounting for almost a full quarter of global economic development over this time period. The percentage of people in China with access to electricity increased from 92 percent in 1992 to 100 percent in 2015.

10　"World Bank Open Data," Open Data (World Bank, January 7, 2020), https://data.worldbank.org/.

These groups of people in China, India, and Africa are likely to fuel much of the growth in global economic progress over the next decades. It will be a massive logistical challenge to provide electricity and access to modern technology to the rising billions. In cases where governmental or nongovernmental organizations can provide the initial infrastructure to deliver electricity, the economic development that comes from electrical infrastructure and access to digital networking will enable these people to pay for their infrastructure, contribute to the global economy, and enjoy a higher standard of living.

At the global level, policymakers and researchers know that development will involve providing access to electricity to the billion people who currently lack access. Governments of many developing countries have made access to electricity a core part of their platforms, and modern history is full of politicians jumpstarting their careers with electricity (or losing their careers because of policy-created energy crises like the unfortunate case of Gray Davis, Governor of California—who is one of only two US governors to ever be recalled from office early—who presided over the Californian Electricity Crisis[11]). One of the most successful public works programs in the United States, The Tennessee Valley Authority Public Utility, was a Depression-era New Deal program from President Roosevelt.[12]

---

11   Robert Salladay, "STATE OF TRANSITION/End of the Davis Era/ Tempered Temperament Led State," SFGate (San Francisco Chronicle, January 15, 2012), https://www.sfgate.com/politics/article/STATE-OF-TRANSITION-End-of-the-Davis-era-2549307.php).

12   "The TVA Act," TVA (Tennessee Valley Authority), accessed January 12, 2020, https://www.tva.gov/About-TVA/Our-History/The-TVA-Act.

The third point in the Energy Trilemma is sustainability. An energy source must be sufficiently sustainable, or dependence on that source will have long-term costs and risks far greater than the simple cost of acquisition and consumption. Current global energy consumption is reasonably affordable and accessible but not sustainable: technically recoverable global oil and coal reserves—the reserves that we know could be acquired regardless of price—are adequate to last for several hundred years and at least several decades at current prices (assuming geopolitical conflicts don't get in the way). Peak oil is not a major concern this century, though the price of new exploration and recovery of more difficult resources can be expected to increase as easy-to-access hydrocarbon conventional reserves are depleted.

These hydrocarbons emit large amounts of carbon dioxide and other pollutants. This carbon-caused climate change is a much more pressing issue than the long-term supply of oil: peak carbon has come long before peak oil.

Direct air pollution is a bigger concern for many countries, especially developing countries with less strict air quality controls. Unsurprisingly, low air quality has been statistically correlated with poor health in China[13] and has been estimated by the RAND Corporation to have cost 6.5 percent of the total Chinese GDP between 2000 and 2010.[14] Emissions

---

13   W. Liu, Z. Xu, and T. Yang, 2018. "Health Effects of Air Pollution in China." *International Journal of Environmental Research and Public Health*, 1471.

14   Keith Crane and Zhimin Mao. Costs of Selected Policies to Address Air Pollution in China. RAND Corporation, 2015. Accessed January 12, 2020.

from industry, transportation, and electrical generation are the primary drivers of air pollution, but one source is responsible for more of the health impact: cooking.

Cooking requires energy in the form of heat. Providing that energy from chemical sources like wood, coal, or other biomass sources can release air pollutants, especially if the combustion of these fuels occurs openly or in low-efficiency stoves. If this cooking happens indoors, the volatiles and particulate matter can radically decrease air quality and increase the incidence of poor health and health conditions.

Nearly three billion people lack access to clean cooking fuel and/or technologies. This has an adverse impact on individual and aggregate health, which will reduce growth in quality of life and economic activity. This lack of access to sustainable cooking will exacerbate inequality: those wealthy enough to have access to clean cooking will avoid the costs associated with the health risks caused by indoor air pollution, while those unable to afford clean cooking will bear a disproportionately large burden of the health costs. It is hard to get out of poverty and even harder to do so when dealing with poor health and increasing environmental pollution.

EXAMPLES

These three points of the Energy Trilemma—access, affordability, and sustainability—show up for almost every analysis or organizational framework that takes a wide view of energy policy. From the US Navy to the UN and British think tanks to the Chinese government, these are the dimensions that energy policies and technologies must be evaluated on.

The US Navy's Energy Security Framework has three pillars for evaluating electrical energy security:

1. Resiliency, "the capability to recover from utility failures,"
2. Reliability, "the capability to resist utility failures," and
3. Efficiency, "the capability to reduce demand and cost for utilities."[15]

The US Navy identifies access to energy as a critical requirement to maintain their capabilities, and diversified and efficient use of energy sources as a force multiplier.[16] Energy is needed to propel warships, and having better energy sources provides a strategic advantage against adversaries. The history of naval warfare is littered with examples of battles and wars that were won because of an energy advantage. The history of technological warfare is fueled by energy.

The Dutch defeated the English repeatedly during the Little Ice Age because of their wind advantage.[17] The English oil-fueled Grand Fleet gained a crucial advantage over the German coal-burning High Seas Fleet at the Battle of Jutland in the First World War because oil provided greater speed and range. Winston Churchill was so convinced of

---

15   US Navy, "Keeping Our Sights on Target: A Strategic Vision for Energy Security," Navy Live (Navy Live, February 2, 2018), https://navylive.dodlive.mil/2018/02/02/keeping-our-sights-on-target-a-strategic-vision-for-energy-security/.

16   "Energy," Dept. of Navy—Energy, Environment, and Climate Change, accessed January 12, 2020, https://navysustainability.dodlive.mil/energy/.

17   Dagomar Degroot, *The Frigid Golden Age: Climate Change, the Little Ice Age, and the Dutch Republic, 1560-1720* (Cambridge, United Kingdom: Cambridge University Press, 2019).

the advantages of oil that he said that the British needed to base their "naval supremacy upon oil" despite the total lack of domestic oil supplies, which meant that switching the Royal Navy to rely on fuel oil instead of coal was "to take arms against a sea of troubles."[18]

Likewise, in the Second World War, British Spitfires were propelled by 100-octane gasoline, which gave them a critical edge in the furious Battle of Britain against the 87-octane-fueled German Messerschmitts. Halfway across the world, in the naval air combat between the United States and Imperial Japan, combat was decided by the skill of pilots and quality of machines, but the US pilots had better fuel—higher octane aviation gasoline—which allowed them to fly farther and faster than their Japanese counterparts over the vast Pacific Ocean.[19]

For development, these three points of the Trilemma also show up. The United Nation's Sustainable Development Goals include Goal Seven: affordable and clean energy, which is to "ensure access to affordable, reliable, sustainable, and modern energy for all." This goal's primary sub-goals are: to increase global access to electricity to 100 percent of the total population by 2030; to provide universal access to clean cooking fuels and technologies by 2030; to substantially increase the share of renewable energy in the global energy mix by 2030; and to double the improvement rate of energy efficiency by 2030.

---

18 Daniel Yergin, *The Prize: the Epic Quest for Oil, Money & Power* (London: Simon & Schuster, 2012), 16.

19 Daniel Yergin, *The Prize: the Epic Quest for Oil, Money & Power* (London: Simon & Schuster, 2012), 157.

The 2016 Sustainable Development Goals report to the General Assembly noted that Goal Seven was critical and that:

"Energy is crucial for achieving almost all of the Sustainable Development Goals, from its role in the eradication of poverty through advancements in health, education, water supply and industrialization, to combating climate change." [20]

Overall, The Energy Trilemma has shown up time and time again in energy policy. Modern solutions to the issue of climate change must be equal or better to conventional hydrocarbon energy sources on account of reliable access, affordable total cost, and sustainable long-term viability. If new energy sources are not better than the sources and technologies that we are dependent on, they will be rejected.

---

20   (UN Economic and Social Council 2016)

2

THE GLOBAL DEPENDENCE ON ENERGY

———

If we could produce electric effects of the required quality, this whole planet and the conditions of existence on it could be transformed. The sun raises the water of the oceans and winds drive it to distant regions where it remains in a state of most delicate balance. If it were in our power to upset it when and wherever desired, this mighty life-sustaining stream could be at will controlled. We could irrigate arid deserts, create lakes and rivers and provide motive power in unlimited amounts. This would be the most efficient way of harnessing the sun to the uses of man.

—NIKOLA TESLA, *MY INVENTIONS*

Before exploring the future of energy production and consumption, I believe it is helpful to understand our current dependence on energy. This chapter looks at the way energy is critical for current civilization and how much of the quality of life and technology we use daily is contingent on constant access to energy. Energy use increases our standard of living and should not be overly demonized.

Understanding the benefits of our current energy consumption is important because any solution to decarbonize our planetary civilization must provide at least the same level of benefits to be accepted. If a solution to reduce carbon emissions requires a substantially reduced standard of living or a lower quality of life, it is unlikely to gather much support in any country. If a solution is substantially more expensive than the status quo, businesses and organizations will be slow to adopt it. A solution must be competitive when the total benefits and costs are compared to what we have today.

THE BENEFITS OF ENERGY DEPENDENCE

Modern civilization is completely dependent on energy. We use energy for lighting, cooking, heating, cooling, transportation, communications, recreation, and manufacturing. Without fuel and electricity, the world economy would instantly collapse, probably killing several billion people. All information and knowledge currently stored in purely digital formats would be lost without electricity to retrieve it. We derive tremendous benefits from our use of energy but become dependent on it in the process. Let's look at some of the ways we benefit and how much we stand to lose without this energy.

Without energy, hospitals can't keep the lights on or instruments sterilized, and medical equipment ceases to function.

Other types of life support and safety-critical systems fail. Modern buildings become almost uninhabitable without energy: no lights, water, heating, ventilation, air conditioning systems, or elevators. Most buildings above a few stories in most parts of the world would be unappealing or unsafe to live in without energy.

Without energy, the most advanced transportation systems become inoperable: no fuel for airplanes and motor vehicles, no electricity for trains or Segways, and in the long run, limited food to power bicycles. Reducing transportation options to only those powered by humans and animals would cripple the modern economy and cause famine on a global scale. Without fast transportation and refrigeration, modern supply lines for food transportation are entirely inoperable at every step in the farm to table process.

Without energy to cook and prepare food using electrical appliances, modern cooking would be impossible. Without energy in some form, all cooking is impossible. Without electricity or gas, the remaining options for cooking energy are wood, coal, and biomass, none of which modern dwellings are designed to use. Cooking food indoors using any of these fuel sources releases carcinogenic air pollution—this would be especially true in unpowered modern buildings without powered HVAC systems—and would be hazardous to human life.

Without energy for refrigeration, most kinds of food become extremely difficult to store. Some foods can be salted or smoked, but the majority of fresh foods would be uneconomical to sell without refrigeration. Many foods currently eaten in preserved forms are difficult to make without refrigeration, due to the short window of time from harvest to preservation before food rots.

Without fuel, all agricultural products that are planted or harvested using tractors and combine harvesters would be harvested by hand or rot in the field. Without fuel, transportation would have to be done entirely by human or animal power, severely limiting the distance food can be transported from farms. Likewise, without power during transportation, food could not be refrigerated, severely limiting the amount of time food can spend in transit, further limiting the distance food can travel. Without refrigeration, most people would lose access to fresh fruit and vegetables, meat, and fish. The majority of farms in the United States would be unable to sell most of their output, which would be further limited because fertilizer is almost never sourced locally. Most fertilizer is also produced from hydrocarbons or using ammonium fixing, which requires large amounts of energy. Without fertilizer and fast mechanized harvesting, yields would fall substantially.

Global crop yields would drop substantially without mechanization, and without motorized transportation and refrigeration, the remaining yields would be difficult to deliver, increasing the amount of food spoiled in transit. The lack of powered transport is made worse by the lack of communication technology. Without energy, modern communication systems are reduced to the Pony-Express era postal service. Fast and cheap digital communications allow farmers to coordinate prices and logistics at the speed of light, allowing for decreased risk. If communication was limited to the speed of horses or bicycles, farmers would be limited in their ability to arrange logistics and acquire supplies. Not being able to determine demand for their agricultural products and current prices through a phone call or Internet search would also increase the risk that they send unwanted or oversupplied goods to market and are unable to turn a profit.

This hypothetical loss of communications technology—no radio, telephone, or Internet—would destroy the world economy. It would become extremely slow to order food, supplies, and consumer products. Most modern services and companies would be unable to operate without these communication technologies—not to mention the lack of electricity required to run any manufacturing equipment, payment systems, or computers—and would be unable to coordinate global operations in any meaningful sense, given the typical speed of the sail-powered ships needed to carry physical mail across oceans.

To illustrate how fast intercontinental transportation would be in a world without powered transportation, the fastest racing sail-powered ships reach average speeds of 30-plus knots (60km/h) under optimal conditions, with the record for fastest twenty-four-hour average being 37.8 knots (43.5 mph / 69kmh).[21] Theoretically, a world-record-breaking racing ship could deliver a letter or small package across the Pacific in a week. However, these racing yachts are not designed to carry any meaningful amount of cargo or mail and cannot stand up to the storms that are likely to

---

21   "24 Hour Distance Records," World Sailing Record Council, accessed January 12, 2020, https://www.sailspeedrecords.com/24-hour-distance).

be experienced when crossing oceans. They also only can reach their top speeds under perfect conditions and are likely to average much slower speeds. There are a handful of racing ships and crews that might be able to deliver priority mail across the Pacific Ocean from the US to China or Japan in three to four weeks, but a more reasonable ship would take ten to twenty weeks to deliver news and communications. This delay would be both ways. A few seconds delay in response on a Skype video call makes it hard to communicate, but a world without energy makes that sound unbelievably fast!

Without electricity, our computers would be reduced to useless chunks of metal, plastic, and silicon. Without computers, modern payment systems do not function. Without credit cards and digital point-of-sale systems, modern economic activity would stop almost entirely.

This dependence on energy is not a modern development: numerous civilizations across all recorded human history have been dependent on energy and have experienced shortages. Some historians even attribute the decline and fall of the Roman Empire to energy shortages. The Industrial Revolution was partially caused by an energy shortage in sixteenth-century Britain: most of the country was deforested for charcoal production, leading to the burning of coal for cooking and refining metals.[22] This happened despite coal being rarer and less clean than wood and charcoal. Most types of coal don't burn cleanly and release a large amount

---

22   John Nef, "An Early Energy Crisis and Its Consequences," *Scientific American*, 1977, 140–151.

of sulfur dioxide and other air pollutants, which can actually damage many industrial products and machines if not treated correctly, in addition to being hazardous to human health. A look at almost all pre-industrial society will show concerns about the cost of fuel for cooking and the cost of feeding animals for transportation.

Overall, the entire planet—developed economies especially so—is completely dependent on energy. This is not inherently bad, as energy consumption allows for increased quality of human life and the economic growth that advances technology and culture, but it has costs and risks. There are costs and risks to reliance on any resource, but the costs and risks of energy dependence are especially high given how critical it is for our use of all other resources.

THE PATH DEPENDENCY OF OUR MACHINES

In addition to modern civilization being dependent on energy, most of our machines that use energy are dependent on a specific fuel or form of energy and require a constant supply to be operated reliably. Most machines use just a single type of fuel, and it is expensive and time-consuming to modify them to accept another. This has implications when designing and purchasing equipment, as the risk of energy prices changing could make a project economically unfeasible.

The requirement to have continuous access to a particular energy source, especially ones that require lengthy transportation like oil, is common when a machine or energy-consuming process is optimized for that specific form of energy.

Gasoline and diesel are similar liquid hydrocarbon fuels derived from crude oil, but a gasoline engine cannot burn diesel and will not operate if you try and run it on diesel. A typical gasoline internal combustion engine can tolerate many impurities in fuel at the cost of reduced performance and increased maintenance needs. For economic and environmental reasons—not to mention effective lobbying by the corn industry—most gasoline in the US is 10 to 15 percent ethanol. Modern gasoline engines work just fine on this blended fuel, but if you put E85—85 percent ethanol, 15 percent gasoline—into a gasoline engine, certain rubber seals and gaskets will dissolve with long-term usage.

Most aircraft engines have strict normal operating requirements for fuel type, despite being able to accommodate a large range of fuels. Most piston planes can run on automotive gasoline, but several unfortunate pilots have learned fatal lessons from putting E10 automotive gasoline into planes with rubber fuel lines (certain rubbers will expand before dissolving in E10, which causes the fuel line to swell up and prevent fuel from flowing). Most jet engines use jet fuel as a lubricant—sometimes as a hydraulic fluid for the engine's internal hydraulic systems—and cannot run on high octane aviation gasoline for long without having parts burn up. Usually, a jet engine must be inspected after twenty to one hundred hours of operation on gasoline, and sometimes must be rebuilt entirely, making gas an expensive emergency fuel.

Electrical generation equipment can run off a number of different energy sources, but most thermal plants are built to consume a single type of fuel for three economic reasons. The first reason is that it is expensive to have the equipment to burn multiple fuel sources because it effectively requires building and maintaining two power plants! The equipment to burn natural gas efficiently is different from the equipment needed to burn coal efficiently. Some types of boilers for steam generation are capable of burning almost anything—oil, coal, biomass, even trash!—but these fuel-agnostic boilers usually require more maintenance, emit more pollution, and are less efficient than more advanced designs. Some advanced steam generation plants use circulating fluidized bed (CFB) boiler designs that can accommodate almost any solid fuel, but these are expensive compared to conventional boilers.

The second reason that electrical generators are built for a specific fuel is the cost of that fuel. For most power plants, the total cost of a particular fuel source will be lower than most others, usually due to proximity. Historically, many power plants have been built near their fuel sources to reduce the cost of transportation. For the typical "mine-mouth" coal plant that is right next to a coal mine, the transportation costs will make most other fuels far more expensive.

The third reason is equipment optimization. Most equipment is designed for a specific type and quality of fuel, to be run under a certain range of conditions. Running equipment on the wrong quality of fuel can cause damage: unexpectedly high levels of sulfur or silica particles in coal can cause damage to a plant[23], decrease efficiency, or increase exhaust pollution to an unacceptable level. In turbines running on natural gas, the methane content of the fuel can vary, and in

---

23   Una Nowling, "Leveraging Fuel Flexibility for Coal Power Plant Survival," *POWER Magazine, September 1, 2015, https://www.powermag. com/leveraging-fuel-flexibility-for-coal-power-plant-survival/.*

some cases where butane, propane, and ethane have not been removed, the turbine will lose efficiency, and when running on severely methane-deficient natural gas, combustion may even be extinguished, resulting in damage.

When possible, it is expensive and slow to switch energy sources for equipment that was not designed to accept multiple fuels. This switching cost for equipment, especially for vehicles and electrical power generation, has strategic security implications for most countries. If a country loses access to a particular fuel source during a conflict, it would lose the ability to wage war effectively until it was able to switch fuel sources for the affected assets. Most assets would take years to convert to another fuel source, making such a switch impractical.

CONCLUSION

Looking at how dependent our civilization is on energy, especially fossil hydrocarbons, is depressing within the context of carbon-emission-caused climate change. However, if a low-carbon source of energy could provide the energy we needed at a lower price, we would see rapid adoption as it became a competitive advantage for businesses and consumers to switch to the new power source. Historically, carbon-intense energy sources like coal and biomass have been the lowest-cost option, but there is a ray of hope for zero-carbon renewable energy: the cost decreases seen over the last decade have made wind and solar energy cost-competitive with coal and natural gas. How will these technological changes change or alter our dependence on energy?

3

THE HOPE OF RENEWABLES

The energy transition is possible and it is affordable. It is of utmost importance that we look at the transition not as a burden, but as an opportunity.
—RAINER BAAKE, STATE SECRETARY, GERMAN FEDERAL
MINISTRY FOR ECONOMIC AFFAIRS AND ENERGY

The specter of climate change is looming, but there is a ray of hope amid the smog: renewable energy technologies have gotten substantially cheaper over the last decade. The prices of solar power and wind energy especially have declined by a surprising degree: in many places, solar and wind energy are now cheaper than coal power plants on a levelized lifetime basis. The price decreases of renewable energy, combined with the increasing political will to implement a carbon tax or similar carbon control scheme means that we have an opportunity to switch to sustainable energy sources.

The speed at which renewable energy resources have been deployed is astounding: solar and wind energy resources have been deployed around the world faster than expected by experts and grid operators. The New England Independent Systems Operator (ISO-NE) forecast in 2015 that they would have 1800 megawatts of solar generation by 2023. By the end of 2018, they already had to deal with 2800 megawatts of solar and forecast almost six gigawatts (or 6,000 megawatts) of solar by 2027.[24] New England is better known for snowstorms than solar, which makes this even more surprising.

Solar has come down in price substantially. Solar cells, the raw modules that convert sunlight into voltage and current, are now below one dollar per watt. Ten years ago, in 2009, these cells would have cost nearly ten dollars per watt. In the late 1970s, when solar photovoltaic cells first became commercially available, they cost more than seventy-five dollars per watt. Solar PV cells are forecast by Wood Mackenzie to decrease in cost to eighteen cents per watt by 2023.[25] At this point, most of the cost of installing a solar photovoltaic system in the United States is spent on installation labor and permit fees.

The cost of electrical generation from wind has also come down by a substantial degree. Onshore renewable wind generation is cheaper than coal in most parts of the United States,

24　ISO New England, 2019, Final 2019 PV Forecast. Holyoke, MA: ISO New England.

25　Jason Deign, "Why PV Costs Have Fallen So Far—and Will Fall Further," Greentech Media, December 14, 2018, https://www.greentechmedia.com/articles/read/why-pv-costs-have-fallen-so-far-and-will-fall-further.

but offshore wind generation remains cost-prohibitive. However, in places like the UK and Denmark, where the wind is plentiful, land costs high, and environmental regulations stringent, offshore wind is extremely competitive with conventional power. The leading wind turbine manufacturing companies in the world are Danish and Chinese. Offshore wind generation still has many logistical complexities that make it more difficult and expensive than onshore wind, but these are also decreasing with scale.

In places where the total cost of wind or solar generation is cheaper than conventional sources, this means that businesses motivated only by their bottom line will build renewable energy instead of fossil-fuel-consuming sources. This can be shifted and incentivized by subsidies or higher environmental standards. Conventional subsidies for renewables like tax credits or cheaper financing have historically worked well to encourage production of renewable energy. Increased environmental standards through stricter regulations increase the cost of polluting, and thus incentivizes the owners of polluting energy assets to reduce emissions. Likewise, investors and utilities considering a new energy resource to provide electricity will take regulatory compliance costs into account during the design and evaluation phases of new projects. They ultimately will prefer different technologies and energy sources depending on the cost of meeting environmental regulations.

Countries like Germany and Japan have created strong economic incentives for individuals, companies, and utilities to invest in energy efficiency projects and renewable energy resources. German investment in wind and solar renewable energy helped encourage Chinese manufacturers to increase the scale of their productions, which decreased manufacturing costs and lowered the costs for solar energy production. German subsidies were so generous that new solar installations in Japan, which was one of the world's leaders in solar installations before Germany's Energy Revolution, dropped almost to zero for a few years while Germany energy producers and individuals were purchasing most of the world's supply of low-cost solar panels.

Likewise, in parts of the United States, wind energy has been cost-competitive with coal in parts of the country for a long time from state and federal incentives. Texas, classic "Big Oil" country, now has more economic activity and jobs in the wind and solar industries than from the oil and classical energy sector.

REGULATION: FAIR PRICING FOR CARBON

One extremely successful policy was the sulfur emissions cap-and-trade bill that helped decrease acid rain in the United States. This regulatory scheme gave sulfur-emitting industries credits based on their current sulfur emissions and then allowed companies to reduce their sulfur air pollution and sell the unneeded credits to companies that were unable or unwilling to reduce their emissions. The total amount of emittable sulfur was reduced by shrinking the total number of credits available and imposing heavy fines on companies that did not buy enough credits to offset their emissions. This provided a financial incentive to reduce sulfur emissions: a company that reduced their emissions faster than mandated by law would have an excess amount of credits they could sell, which provided a revenue stream from investments in pollution controls. These incentives were so successful that a surplus of sulfur credits were created, the cost of credits remained affordable for companies that faced a difficult and expensive process of reducing their emissions, and the total amount of sulfur emissions and acid rain decreased substantially.

This example of a successful cap-and-trade plan for airborne emissions and air pollution has been a model and inspiration for market-based carbon emission control regulatory schemes. A properly enforced and accounted for tax of ten to two hundred dollars per ton of emitted CO_2 would solve global warming. Various estimates of the costs and benefits of a carbon tax put the optimal number between forty and one hundred dollars per ton. Cap-and-trade-style emissions reduction schemes allow companies and individuals to make choices based on price signals instead of green perception and moral judgments. Optimization is simultaneously easy and hard. Finding the maximum or minimum for a function of a variable is a known math and engineering problem and in most single variable cases is usually straightforward.

Take the example of an investor considering the opportunity to invest in a new power plant construction project. The investor's goal is to maximize their profit—their return on investment—and so they find all the variables that influence cost and profits and try to find the combinations of variables that maximize their total return on investment. They can decide to either maximize their total profit regardless of investment size or to maximize their rate of return. They may be faced with the decision to build a $100-million power plant that will provide a total return of $200 million over its expected lifetime for a total profit of $100 million or to build a $20-million power plant that will provide a return of $60 million over its expected lifetime. If they go with the larger plant, they'll make $200 million—a 200 percent return on their initial investment. The smaller plant will make them $60 million, or a 300 percent return on investment. If they can only build one and all other details are equal—expected investment length, risks, etc.—then the investor will have to decide whether they want to make the most money possible or get the best return on their investment. They are forced to trade off one desirable outcome (making a larger sum of money) and another desirable outcome (having a larger return on investment). These trade-offs are what make optimization in decision-making hard.

Sometimes optimization is easy: when a company wants to be environmentally-friendly and profitable, and its cheapest energy source is renewable energy, the decision to avoid conventional energy sources is easy. When they are forced to trade cost for environmental friendliness, that decision gets harder. Sometimes, if a decision would be close, such as a renewable zero-carbon energy that costs 5 percent more than conventional alternatives, the nonmonetary variable wins out. But when environmentally-friendly decisions start becoming cost-prohibitive, most companies will switch toward cheaper options. The threshold where this trade-off occurs is different for every company. Some companies are willing to pay 50 percent or more for clean energy and write it off as a marketing expense so they can use their sustainability as a competitive advantage when communicating their values to their customers. Other companies would rather go bankrupt before paying 1 percent more for green energy. If the cost of carbon emissions were included in conventional power generation, companies that are primarily motivated by profits would switch faster when the prices of all options included externalities like carbon emissions.[26]

There would be drawbacks to these taxes, but most of these drawbacks are common to other emissions-control schemes. Cap-and-trade schemes are generally regarded as some of the most flexible and effective regulatory schemes to reduce the emissions of specific air pollutants.

The best part of emissions-control regulations is that the threat of regulation is enough to reduce investment in conventional carbon-emitting energy resources. The financial and regulatory analysts who plan and price these renewable projects are quite intelligent and will attempt to quantify the risk of potentially costly regulation. For a coal power plant that has an expected lifetime of twenty to fifty years, there is plenty of time for emissions requirements to become more expensive. If a cap-and-trade regulatory scheme was introduced during the lifetime of that plant, it would cost more to operate that plant: either the plant operators would have to purchase emissions credits to offset their emissions, or they

---

26   I once heard an anecdote about an accountant describing climate change as the biggest accounting failure of human history. Carbon emissions are free: there is no cost to carbon dioxide emissions when you emit them. When the amount of greenhouse gases and carbon dioxide in the atmosphere increase, costs for everyone increase. The costs of climate change are an externality of greenhouse gas emissions that the emitters don't have to directly pay. Adding this cost to emissions forces emitters to pay an accurate price, allowing for better market forces to operate.

would need to invest in emissions-reduction technology and improvement, which could be extremely expensive.

The global push to decrease carbon emissions and reduce the risk of catastrophic climate change is increasing the willingness to implement carbon taxes to accurately reflect the true cost of our energy. This greater chance of carbon control, combined with the tremendous cost decreases of renewable energy technologies, gives us a real chance of being able to keep global warming to two degrees or less of warming.

RENEWABLE ENERGY CREDITS

One of the strangest and most interesting combinations of different policies is free solar energy in Washington, DC: Kyle Yost and his company, DC Solar, LLC, will install solar panels on your roof for free if you own a home in DC and pay federal income taxes.

How is this possible?

Solar Renewable Energy Credits (SRECs) and a goal of 100 percent renewable energy by 2032.

If you generate electricity from solar sources in Washington, DC, you earn one SREC per megawatt-hour of electricity generated. If you sell electricity within Washington, DC, you must generate a certain percent of your total energy from solar or pay a penalty. Electrical providers in DC also have a third option: purchase SRECs to cover their generation. Many states and countries have SRECs and requirements to have a certain number of credits per megawatt-hour generated, but DC is unique in how land-constrained the city is: DC is a small and well-developed area, meaning that there are not many good locations to put up a large solar farm. Limited space for large-scale solar development and growing requirements to generate a relatively large amount of electricity from solar—the target was raised in 2019 to 10 percent of total generation coming from solar by 2041—has led to a lucrative market for SRECs in DC.

The value of these SRECs increases the expected total value of a residential solar panel above just the cost savings from generating electricity. If you're paying the average of $0.13 per kilowatt-hour (kWh) in DC, a solar installation that generates 10,000 kWh over the year would save you from buying $1,300 of electricity. This solar installation would also generate 10 SRECs that currently have a market value of $300–$400 each—and $300–$400 looks like a pretty good deal to electricity providers when the Solar Alternative Compliance Payment is $500 per megawatt-hour.

The renewable credits generated by a solar installation in Washington, DC, are more valuable than the electricity they produce.

These solar installations are still expensive and are not guaranteed to be a good investment—except for the 30 percent discount from the federal government's Investment Tax Credit (ITC) that can make residential and commercial solar an excellent investment. This policy allows an individual or business to claim 30 percent of the total cost of a solar installation as a tax credit on their federal income taxes. Minus the low costs of having an accountant double-check everything, this means that solar panels in most cases are 30 percent cheaper than they would be. This does not reduce the value of the electricity they generate or any other incentives such as SRECs.

In exchange for the cash that a homeowner will get back from the ITC tax rebate and the right to sell the SRECs, DC Solar will effectively install solar panels for free and earn their profit by selling the SRECs. This is a unique business opportunity that would not exist without these policies.

Business opportunities like these are being created all over the world as the economics of renewable energy generation improve faster than anyone expected. The amount of zero-carbon generation being installed around the world deserves attention and should be explored further.

4

RENEWABLES FALL SHORT

———

Le mieux est l'ennemi du bien.
The perfect is the enemy of the good.
—VOLTAIRE, *DICTIONNAIRE PHILOSOPHIQUE*

With the costs of renewables falling so quickly, the planet now has a clear and nearly affordable path forward toward generating 100 percent of our energy from zero-emissions renewable energy technologies. Except we can't replace fossil fuel plants with just wind or solar. Wind and solar are variable energy sources—they provide energy only when the wind is blowing or the sun is shining. Current electrical demand is not especially flexible, which leads to issues when a large portion of total energy is generated from intermittent variable sources. Given that electrical generation and load must be balanced for the grid to be stable—supply must almost exactly match demand—either generation or demand must be flexible. If demand is inflexible, then there must be some flexible resources that can be dispatched to balance supply and demand and prevent blackouts, and intermittent sources like wind and solar cannot provide that flexibility on their own.

One of these issues is reduced consumption of non-solar resources in areas with large residential solar installations. Visualizing net electrical load in regions with a large amount of residential solar energy looks like a duck.

THE DUCK CURVE

The Duck Curve—Jordan Wirfs-Brock[27]

In 2008, researchers at the National Renewable Energy Lab (NREL) predicted that Solar Photovoltaic costs were declining

---

27   Jordan Wirfs-Brock, "Why Is California Trying to Behead The Duck?" Inside Energy, October 26, 2016, http://insideenergy.org/2014/10/02/ie-questions-why-is-california-trying-to-behead-the-duck/.

rapidly, which would lead to widespread adoption and challenges to existing electricity utilities.[28] In 2013, the California Independent Systems Operator (CAISO) published a report showing how the early effects of PV adoption were reducing normal midday energy consumption and predicted that this reduction would increase over the next decade. The curve charted prominently in the report looked like a duck, leading to "The Duck Curve" being a term used frequently in serious technical and policy debates about integrating renewable energy into the grid.

Conventional electrical consumption usually peaks between 8:00 and 11:00 a.m. as people start their day, declines slightly during the afternoon and then has a second, even higher peak consumption from 5:00 to 8:00 p.m. After the evening peak, electricity use falls to a minimum between about 12:00 a.m. and 5:00 a.m., where the only consumption is background consumption and twenty-four-hour industrial consumption. Most electricity consumption coincides with aggregate personal activity.

Distributed solar PV changes this equation.

When solar energy resources are installed on a building, that building's total energy consumption does not change. The energy consumed first, however, will be from the solar panels on the roof. This leads to the building's demand for external energy decreasing while the solar panels are producing, and if solar production exceeds demand, the building will turn

---

28 National Renewable Energy Laboratory, 2008, Production Cost Modeling for High Levels of Photovoltaics Penetration, Midwest Research Institute.

into a net energy producer. If there are incentives to feed energy back into the electrical grid, such as net metering or feed-in tariffs, it can become profitable to oversize a solar array to produce far more energy than a building consumes.[29]

When enough buildings reduce consumption during peak daylight hours or even start exporting energy to the grid operators, this looks like a large reduction in demand from about 8:00 a.m. to 6:00 p.m. depending on the time of year. With large numbers of solar PV installations, this changes the minimum electrical consumption to 1:00 p.m. to 2:00 p.m. instead of 1:00 a.m. to 3:00 a.m.! This production helps reduce daytime carbon emissions but creates three large challenges: the evening ramp (the neck of the duck), overgeneration and curtailment (the belly of the duck), and reduced stability and frequency control.

THE DUCK'S NECK—THE EVENING RAMP

Dealing with a large and fast increase in electrical demand is challenging, and the size and speed of the evening increase are magnified by the high penetration of solar PV. Peak solar production starts declining around 3:00 p.m., and peak energy consumption usually peaks around 6:00 p.m. to 7:00 p.m. This means from 3:00 p.m. to 6:00 p.m., utilities with a high penetration of behind the meter solar PV must increase their production from minimum to maximum, which is not

---

29 My cousin has told a story about friends of friends in San Diego who reportedly purchased heavily discounted solar panels at solar installer bankruptcy auctions, installed them at their own house to take advantage of the net-metering policies, and were receiving a check instead of a bill every month from the utility.

easy when some conventional thermal plants can take hours to start or stop safely. CAISO's updated 2016 report on the duck chart shows that predictions were actually conservative and that the evening ramp is getting steeper faster than expected. "The duck chart shows the system requirement to supply an additional 13,000 megawatt (MW), all within approximately three hours, to replace the electricity lost by solar power as the sun sets."[30] Thirteen thousand MW is equivalent to the output of thirteen large nuclear power plants—or, for fans of *Back to The Future*, enough power to send McFly's DeLorean back in time ten times.

This massive demand for increased electricity over a short period of time is difficult for conventional power plants to meet. These thermal plants that are a part of the "long-start" resources that make up a large portion of the grid's baseload power supply require a long time to start or stop. A conventional coal plant can take four or more hours to reach peak output and cannot reduce output much faster. This means that most of the upswing in generation will need to come from non-baseload sources.

Of these non-baseload-sources, open-cycle gas plants are the traditional go-to supply for increases in electrical consumption because they can start to increase output within minutes instead of hours. The trade-off is that they are much less efficient and more expensive than combined-cycle gas plants, which results in higher costs for electricity and much higher carbon emissions.

---

30 California Independent System Operator, 2016, "What The Duck Curve Tells us about Managing a Green Grid," Folsom: CAISO.

To deal with this evening ramp, utilities will need to become more flexible about how they produce electricity and encourage their customers to consume electricity at times that are more beneficial to the grid. Utilities need to strangle the duck curve.

THE BODY OF THE DUCK—CURTAILMENT

The second challenge caused by the duck curve and the high penetration of solar PV is that of overgeneration and curtailment. If there is too much solar energy being fed into the grid, utilities may be forced to either curtail some renewable energy and temporarily prohibit it from being added into the grid or be forced to reduce the price of energy to below zero to increase consumption. Because supply and demand must exactly match in an electrical grid, if there is too much renewable supply, steps must be taken to balance that equation.

Consider a nuclear power plant. Nuclear power plants are generally run close to maximum design capacity for long periods of time. Once constructed, nuclear power plants are a low-carbon way to provide electricity at all hours of the day. They are also some of the slowest responding resources currently operating on the grid today, but in many markets, they are essential for providing baseload power. If a nuclear power plant is running and a utility is forced to choose between shutting that nuclear plant off and using more solar for a few minutes, they will almost always choose to curtail that solar generation.

Much of this solar curtailment will occur in favor of conventional hydrocarbon resources—the ones needed to meet the evening ramp—and will decrease the amount of electricity generated from solar, increasing the costs and carbon emissions of the grid.

THE FLAPPING OF WINGS—VOLTAGE INSTABILITY

The third challenge of the duck curve is grid stability and frequency control. Most behind-the-meter solar PV follows the frequency of the grid. If the amount of energy from solar becomes large compared to the energy from conventional sources that provide that base frequency, the frequency of the grid becomes able to fluctuate dangerously fast. These fluctuations are dangerous because if the frequency of the grid deviates too much from the norm, it will cause blackouts.

If using all the solar energy generated would reduce the number of generators providing frequency control ancillary services (FCAS) to dangerously low levels, utilities will curtail that renewable generation.

Utilities can solve these challenges by incentivizing more flexible energy resources: faster start conventional resources, smarter consumption with demand response and time-of-use pricing, and energy storage. With large-scale energy storage, the duck curve changes from a shape that induces nightmares in grid operators to a shape in the data worth chuckling about.

The duck curve shows one of the biggest challenges of increased generation from renewable resources. Flexibility and dispatchable resources are needed to generate 100 percent of total electricity from renewable sources. Traditionally, these flexible and responsive resources have been natural gas peaking plants, but resources like that, which are powered by hydrocarbon fuels, emit greenhouse gases, which make them mostly incompatible with a zero-emissions electrical grid.

To generate all of our electricity from renewable resources, we'll need some that are flexible and responsive. Some of these, like biomass and hydropower, are excellent resources. Not all regions are suitable for hydro or large-scale biomass, which means some other source of dispatchable energy is needed.

Overall, renewable energy resources alone are not enough to satisfy modern energy consumption. Progressive regions of the world that are approaching high levels of renewable penetration are starting to experience the challenges that come from transitioning to low-carbon energy sources. The utilities of the past forecasted demand and dispatched generation and now will have to forecast generation and try their best to dispatch demand. There are two good solutions to this transition: energy storage and virtual power plants.

5

ENERGY STORAGE – HALF THE SOLUTION

—

Storage, whatever forms it will take in the end, is not the holy grail because it helps to balance the grid we have (though this is the story we tell ourselves). It's the holy grail because it allows us to build an electric world that functions otherwise, that has the flexibility to move and change with whatever the twenty-first century will throw at us.

—GRETCHEN BAKKE, *THE GRID*

LIGHTNING DOWN UNDER

On August 25, 2018, thirty-nine seconds after 1:11 p.m., a lightning strike caused the Queensland-New South Wales Interconnection to trip, separating Queensland from the National Electrical Market. The connector had been importing 978 Megawatts at the time of the disruption and losing this capacity—the equivalent of a full-sized nuclear power plant—caused the electrical grid's frequency to start falling below 50 Hz. At 49.85 Hz, the Hornsdale Power Reserve in South Australia—the largest lithium-ion battery facility in the world[31]—switched from charging to discharging to restore normal frequency. The Tesla-built energy storage facility switched from charging at 37 MW to discharging at 50 MW in a few hundred milliseconds, slowing the rate of change of frequency. This large shift from electrical consumer to producer continued over the next few seconds as output increased to 84.3 MW. The frequency of the South Australian grid had by this time dropped below 49.2 Hz, causing the Heywood Interconnector between South Australia and Victoria to trip.[32]

South Australia was exporting 430 MW of electricity through the Heywood Interconnect, and the loss of this load caused the now-isolated South Australian grid's frequency to rise dangerously fast due to the oversupply of generation. Large increases in frequency can cause generators or loads to disconnect from the grid to avoid damage, and fast changes that have a high rate of change of frequency are especially difficult for equipment to handle. The frequency of the South Australian grid surpassed 50.15 Hz a few seconds after Heywood tripped and was in danger of going higher. The price of electricity, which had been averaging between $70 per megawatt hour and $100 per megawatt hour, went negative due to the oversupply of electricity and reached -$1,000 per megawatt hour. The grid briefly was

31   Neoen, 2019, Hornsdale Power Reserve, accessed December 10, 2019, https://hornsdalepowerreserve.com.au/.

32   Australian Energy Market Operator, 2018, Preliminary Report— Queensland and South Australia System Separation on 25 August 2018, AEMO.

paying people to consume electricity to avoid a blackout due to oversupply. The Hornsdale Power Reserve began charging at a rate of 20 MW for a few seconds until the South Australian Grid was safely back within the normal operating range.

Without the Hornsdale Power Reserve acting to maintain grid frequency, it is likely that South Australia's electrical network would have suffered far worse. The engineering consultancy Aurecon estimated that without the additional capacity provided by the Power Reserve, grid frequency would have dropped below 49 Hz, which would have triggered under-frequency load shedding.[33] Load shedding, where electrical loads are disconnected from the grid to reduce demand, is widely used by utilities that are unable to organize adequate supply.[34] When utilities are literally unable to keep the lights on, most engage in load shedding to maintain power to some of their customers. AEMO, the Australian Energy Market Operator, maintains and operates Australia's national electrical grid and engages in two types of load shedding depending on circumstances: automatic load shedding and rotating manual load shedding.

Rotating manual load shedding, also known as rolling blackouts, is used when demand far exceeds supply and the imbalance is known ahead of time. Utilities cut power

---

33   Aurecon, 2019, "Hornsdale Power Reserve Year 1 Technical and Market Impact Case Study," Aurecon.

34   "AEMO: Generators Must Do Better When Grid Wobbles," *Australian Financial Review, January 9, 2019, https://www.afr.com/politics/aemo-generators-must-do-better-when-grid-wobbles-20190109-h19vu9.*

to specific regions or customers and rotate the affected parties until sufficient supply allows all consumers to be supplied. In South Australia, manual load shedding occurs within some number of the twenty-two distinct regions for up to forty-five minutes per region until generation capacity can safely supply the total load. Rotational load shedding occurred in California during the 2001 energy crisis and occurs on a regular basis in some countries. The load shedding in Ghana, Africa, is referred to as "Dumsor" by locals who are rightfully upset by twelve- to twenty-four-hour planned blackouts. Poor management exacerbated by drought in Ghana results in chronic load shedding that is estimated to cost almost $700 million per year in productivity losses, or close to 2 percent of GDP.[35]

Automatic load shedding occurs when frequency or voltage in an electrical network drops below a threshold. Under-frequency load shedding occurs automatically in Australia when the frequency drops below 49 Hz and is one of the last automatic safeguards preventing total grid failure and blackouts. Grid-connected equipment that is configured for under-frequency load shedding disconnects itself when frequency drops below the setpoint, reducing load on the grid and allowing frequency to rise. If frequency continues to fall despite load shedding, blackouts will occur when generators disconnect from the grid to avoid the damage that occurs when they run below frequency. Automatic load shedding and the unplanned disruptions it causes can be expensive, though preferable to full-scale blackouts.

---

35   Center for Global Development, 2017, "The Electricity Situation in Ghana: Challenges and Opportunities," Washington, DC: Center for Global Development.

The Hornsdale facility was critical to preventing automatic load shedding in South Australia by keeping the frequency above 49 Hz and helped reduce the potential for blackouts.[36] Neighboring New South Wales was not quite as lucky because the frequency dropped below 49 Hz, triggering several large industrial consumers to reduce demand by six hundred-plus MW for a period of thirty minutes. In Sydney, forty-five thousand homes were without power for several hours and numerous intersections were left without functioning traffic lights.[37] The chaos and disruption caused by these small-scale blackouts would have been overshadowed by larger-scale blackouts, economic disruption, and the increased risk of loss of human life.

THE BENEFITS OF STORAGE

Energy storage facilities like the Hornsdale Power Reserve provide great value for the electrical grid in emergency situations like the August 25 incident. There are two primary uses of utility-scale energy storage for the electrical grid: backup and peaking, and reducing curtailment.

These primary-use cases provide several benefits. Storage for backup power reduces or eliminates the severity and costs

---

36 Karen Grahm, "Tesla's Big Battery in Australia Has Defied All Expectations," Digital Journal, October 4, 2018, http://www.digitaljournal.com/tech-and-science/technology/tesla-s-big-battery-in-australia-has-defied-all-expectations/article/533773.

37 Joanne Nova, "Report on Aug 25 Blackouts Shows How Fragile Our Grid Is (and the Real Cost of Cheap Solar Panels)," JoNova, January 2019, http://joannenova.com.au/2019/01/report-on-aug-25-blackouts-shows-how-fragile-our-grid-is-and-the-real-cost-of-cheap-solar-panels/.

of many types of emergencies by providing enough reserve power to keep the grid stable until other generation can be brought online or the original issue is resolved. Likewise, enough storage can be used to handle temporary peaks and reduce or eliminate the need to bring other generation online. Storage for backup and peaking makes the grid more reliable and reduces the costs of peak demand.

The frequency-control services that utility-scale storage can provide allow for greater utilization of intermittent renewable energy sources by reducing curtailment. This increases the economic value of those resources and decreases the amount of time that conventional fossil fuel-powered generation has to be used, reducing carbon emissions.

BACKUP AND PEAKING

A small amount of energy storage has the ability to reduce the cost and carbon intensity of the grid to a surprising degree by replacing gas-fired peaking plants. These plants typically have utilization factors of 5 to 6 percent and some are run even less frequently, just a few days or hours a year during the highest demand. During a July heatwave, for example, when the demand for electricity is at a seasonal peak and exacerbated by particularly high demand for air conditioning and cooling due to the weather, demand will be at the highest. During these peak demand periods, peaking power plants will turn on to provide the needed electricity to keep the grid up. This is a valuable service, and wholesale electricity prices rise accordingly.

The benefit of market systems is that they allow resources to be dispatched according to the cost of generation. The downside of market systems is that prices rise when supply is low. Take the Palo Verde price hub in the US Southwest as an example. In 2018, the wholesale price of electricity averaged $70.85 per MWh. The maximum daily price recorded on August 6 was $378/MWh. This price, a factor of five greater than the yearly average, is the daily average for August 6.[38] The five- or fifteen-minute spot prices for electricity can reach $10,000/MWh when demand is so tight that the last few megawatts of generation are the difference between keeping the lights on and a blackout. In cases where energy storage can provide for this peak demand, gas-peaking plants become unnecessary and the total cost of electricity can be reduced.

These gas-peaking plants also have higher emissions per MWh than more efficient power plants, which in turn have higher emissions than zero-carbon renewable energy sources like wind and solar. Gas turbines are usually most efficient at higher temperatures and greater power outputs, so when peaker turbines increase output as fast as possible to match demand, their emissions will be even higher at first than if they were already producing at full capacity.[39] In some cases, combining energy storage with gas peaker plants allows them to operate more efficiently, at lower cost, and with fewer emissions.

---

38 "Wholesale Electricity and Natural Gas Market Data," US Energy Information Administration (EIA) , accessed January 12, 2020, https://www.eia.gov/electricity/wholesale/.

39 Sajith Wijesuriya, "The 'Peakers': The Role of Peaking Power Plants and Their Relevance Today," SciencePolicy circle, accessed January 12, 2020, https://www.sciencepolicycircle.org/38-the-peakers-the-role-of-peaking-power-plants-and-their-relevance-today.

Storage is also being added to existing gas-peaking plants to allow them to start slower. Gas-peaking turbines, like regular gas turbines and most combustion engines, have a relatively narrow range at which they operate most efficiently. Operating outside of this range means that it takes more heat to generate the same amount of electricity. More heat requires more fuel, which increases costs and emissions. A relatively small amount of storage allows a peaking-plant operator to be more flexible without incurring higher costs.

Enough energy storage resources to replace peaking plants would also provide increased resiliency in the form of backup supply and frequency control services. The Hornsdale Power Reserve provides an excellent example of how energy storage improves the quality of the grid by offering bulk storage over long durations, large amounts of power output to meet short-term demand, and frequency control services to keep the grid stable.

CURTAILMENT REDUCTION

As was mentioned in Chapter 7, the curtailment of variable renewable generation is becoming a large issue for grid operators and renewable asset owners. Curtailment is an issue for asset owners because they generally receive less compensation when they produce less energy.

Asset owners usually only get paid when they generate electricity, so they have no incentives to voluntarily curtail their production.

Most renewable energy assets sell energy according to their Power Purchase Agreements (PPA). Generally, these contracts are structured so that energy asset owners are compensated based on the amount of power they generate over the lifetime of the contract. These agreements are usually set up over a fixed term, usually ten to twenty-five years, during which the purchasing party agrees to buy electricity from the selling party—though it should be noted that some utilities are moving toward two- to five-year agreements for renewable energy projects because of how quickly the technological and economic landscape is changing.

When there is an imbalance on the grid, the operators need to adjust generation or demand to bring operations back within normal tolerances. When the issue is excess production, the fastest and most reliable option available is to curtail generation by ordering generators to reduce production or disconnect from the grid. Shutting down conventional thermal generation like coal or gas plants can be slow and expensive, which usually means that renewable generation is the first to be curtailed. Curtailing renewable energy increases overall carbon emissions and is leaving nearly free energy on the table.

Storage can reduce curtailment at the utility-scale by:

- Storing excess energy instead of curtailing that production
- Providing frequency control services to increase grid stability
- Firming renewable output so that it can be dispatched more like a conventional asset.

Reducing renewable curtailment is beneficial because it reduces the cost of electricity and decreases carbon emissions. Energy storage allows curtailment to be reduced.

ENERGY STORAGE: ONLY HALF THE SOLUTION

Energy storage is an important technology that will be pivotal to reducing carbon emissions while increasing overall energy production to raise global standards of living. However, it is likely that energy storage will not be deployed fast enough to solve the global and local energy challenges we are facing. To understand why storage alone will not solve the issue, we need to understand the specific technologies used to store energy.

6

ENERGY STORAGE TECHNOLOGIES

It's still magic even if you know how it's done.
—TERRY PRATCHETT, *A HAT FULL OF SKY*

Being able to store energy for future consumption makes the grid more flexible, which allows for intermittent renewable energy to be fully utilized without the need for conventional hydrocarbon generation to bridge the gap between renewable supply and total demand. Understanding the different types of energy storage technology in operation is important to see how storage currently fits into the electrical grid and how it will fit into the more flexible and distributed electrical grid of the future.

There are as many different ways to store energy as there are different kinds of energy, with the primary types of energy used for storage being chemical, mechanical, electrical, and thermal. Different technologies have different performance in terms of cost, power output, power density, and risks. Even within specific categories of storage technology, there are wide differences in performance depending on the details of implementation.

CHEMICAL STORAGE

Chemical energy storage currently only has a few large-scale commercially used technologies for bulk electrical storage: electrochemical batteries, synthetic fuel synthesis, and hydrogen electrolysis. There are numerous types of batteries used for grid-scale storage and even more kinds used for smaller electronic devices. The synthesis of chemical fuels for energy storage is not currently popular due to high costs and the extremely competitive low cost of fossil fuels.[40] In the future, however, the synthesis of carbon-neutral hydrogen fuel or methane may become popular as a fuel source. For hydrogen production coupled with a gas turbine or hydrogen fuel cell, this could make an effective source of grid-scale energy storage. Currently, batteries are the most popular electrochemical storage.

Batteries are electrochemical devices that store charge by moving ions between an anode and cathode using an electrolyte. In the context of energy storage, batteries refer

---

40 Fossil fuels are a chemical form of energy storage: living plants convert solar energy into stored chemical energy through photosynthesis. Breaking the bonds of carbon dioxide is extremely energy intensive, and when these plants died, the energy they had stored was slowly converted over millions of years into coal, oil, and gas, which are primarily made of hydrocarbons. By burning these fossil fuels, we convert them back into carbon dioxide and water and release the stored energy in the form of heat.

exclusively to secondary batteries that can be recharged hundreds or thousands of times unlike primary batteries, which cannot be recharged. Most battery installations consist of dozens of battery packs, which are made up of thousands or tens of thousands of smaller battery cells. There are many different kinds of battery systems, but because each battery cell is usually small, systems can be highly modular to optimize for the duration of discharge—the total amount of energy stored—or speed of discharge, the maximum power that the system can produce. There are many factors to consider when picking a battery chemistry and system design:

- Specific Energy—kWh/Kilogram
- Energy Density—kWh/Liter
- Charge/Discharge Speed
- Battery Lifetime—Number of charge/discharge cycles before performance is reduced
- Self-discharge Rate—How fast an unused battery loses charge
- Environmental Tolerances—Acceptable temperature/humidity
- Efficiency—Percent of stored energy lost
- Safety
- Cost Per Stored Energy—$/kWh
- Cost Per Power Output—$/kW

All of these factors depend on battery chemistry and system design, as well as a system's operational requirements. Several of these factors are limited by chemistry and the laws of physics: there is a maximum amount of energy released when a lithium atom is oxidized within a battery, which puts a theoretical limit on specific energy given the weight of the chemically relevant materials in a battery. Other factors such as cost and safety are primarily determined by system design, industrial processes, and economies of scale. There are several different types of chemistry that are worth going over.

Lithium-ion batteries are the most common type of electrochemical storage system utilized in the United States and consisted of 85 percent of installed operating battery storage plants in the United States in 2017.[41] Lithium-ion is popular because it is usually the cheapest and fastest option to deploy (Tesla's Hornsdale Power Reserve used lithium-ion batteries). Lithium-ion batteries are energy dense and offer some of the highest performance to weight and performance to size of any commercially available bulk electrochemical storage technologies. These cost reductions have only happened recently, and other storage chemistries and technologies have a great deal of promise.

There are numerous types of lithium-ion battery chemistries, all of which have different performance characteristics and material costs. Some like lithium-polymer batteries are used when performance per weight and performance per volume are prioritized over cost and longevity—though the useful lifetime of a battery can also be improved with better materials and better manufacturing. Most modern personal electronics like phones, tablets, and laptops use lithium-polymer batteries because they offer high-energy densities. By using a dry polymer or polymer-gel electrolyte instead of a liquid electrolyte, the weight and volume are lower and the battery

---

41   US Energy Information Administration—EIA, Form EIA-860 detailed data, accessed January 12, 2020, https://www.eia.gov/electricity/data/eia860/.

can store more energy. These high-energy densities are desirable in all applications—except the Samsung Note 7.

Sodium batteries are the second most popular electrochemical storage technology currently in use, making up 9.5 percent of operational grid-scale battery storage in the United States in 2017. Most of these are molten sodium-sulfur batteries that use the chemical energy released by converting sodium metal into sodium salts. This reversible chemical reaction between sodium and sodium polysulfides (the salts formed when reacting sodium with sulfur) can be used to efficiently store excess energy and has been used with commercial success.

The Presidio Battery Project in Presidio, Texas, was completed in 2010 and has been providing energy storage and voltage regulation services to improve grid stability. This battery has been a commercial success and allowed Electric Transmission Texas, the project's owner, to defer $15 million in infrastructure upgrades by almost ten years.[42] The $25 million 14 MWh molten-sodium sulfur battery received a software upgrade in 2017 to allow it to provide frequency regulation services to the electrical grid, unlocking additional revenue streams for the battery facility.[43] The battery also had enough storage capacity to power the city of Presidio for almost eight hours, which allows the utility to reduce

---

42 Electric Transmission Texas, 2010, "Presidio NAS Battery Project Facts at a Glance," ETTexas.com, accessed December 10, 2019, http://www.ettexas.com/Content/documents/NaSBatteryOverview.pdf.

43 Peter Maloney, "Software Upgrade to Old Sodium Battery Marks Shift in AEP's Storage Strategy," Utility Dive, May 9, 2017, https://www.utilitydive.com/news/software-upgrade-to-old-sodium-battery-marks-shift-in-aeps-storage-strateg/442223/.

maintenance costs and increase safety by switching the city to battery power when doing repairs on the long-distance transmission lines that normally power the city.

Sodium batteries are popular for long-duration storage projects. The United Arab Emirates (UAE) has installed almost 650 MWh of sodium-sulfur batteries.[44] The fifteen storage systems distributed around Abu Dhabi make up 108 MW of total capacity and can be used independently or as a single virtual power plant entity. The investment in storage will allow the UAE to defer investment in new thermal generation—conventional fossil fuel power plants—and will allow diesel generation during peak hours to be reduced while still meeting demand. The sodium-sulfur batteries will also provide frequency regulation, voltage control, and operating reserves to make the grid more stable. Sodium-sulfur batteries were selected for this project because of the lower cost expected for the long term (six hours of operation) discharge requirement and because of sodium sulfur's endurance in hot climates: lithium-ion batteries perform worse by losing efficiency and total capacity in hot weather and age faster when cycled under high temperatures. Using lithium-ion batteries in conditions and climates that are too hot or cold requires additional environmental controls to increase system life and performance, which increases costs and can make them less desirable than sodium-sulfur batteries.

---

44 Andy Colthorpe, "UAE Integrates 648MWh of Sodium Sulfur Batteries in One Swoop," Energy Storage News, January 28, 2019, https://www.energy-storage.news/news/uae-integrates-648mwh-of-sodium-sulfur-batteries-in-one-swoop.

Redox flow batteries are currently deployed in large-scale trial projects in the United States and made up 2.5 percent of storage in 2017. These batteries are almost closer to fuel cells than the classic rechargeable battery cells that resemble larger consumer batteries, as they store the liquid components of the battery in separate tanks and pump them over a membrane to charge or discharge the battery. Flow batteries are exciting because they lack almost all of the disadvantages of lithium-ion and other purely electrochemical batteries: they are generally safer and lose less capacity over time. They are also more flexible because the total storage can be expanded by adding additional liquid storage tanks, which is far cheaper than the new batteries that are required to expand a conventional battery system. The downsides of redox flow batteries is that they generally have lower power capacities, and it is expensive and difficult to increase their power output. The energy density is typically worse than other battery chemistries, which results in larger and heavier systems.

Nickel and lead-acid batteries made up 1.4 percent and 1.2 percent of the total storage capacity of grid-connected electrochemical systems in the United States in 2017. These storage systems are grid-scale pilots. There is only one grid-scale nickel battery currently connected to the grid. The 40 MW/11 MWh Nickel Battery Energy Storage System in Fairbanks, Alaska, was the largest grid-connected battery in the world when it opened in 2003. The system provides enough backup power during power outages so that the Golden Valley Electric Association Utility can start up backup thermal generation to prevent outages. The 1,500-ton battery has an expected lifespan of twenty to thirty years and is still going strong sixteen years into operation: the battery has responded to an average of fifty-two power outages per year since opening, and in 2018 prevented 309,000 Golden Valley customers from losing power during some of the fifty-nine outages the battery responded to.[45]

Lead-acid batteries, like larger versions of the batteries in internal combustion engine-powered vehicles that power the starter motor, have also been used for grid-scale storage. Lead-acid has traditionally had lower performance and far more expensive costs than lithium-ion, as well as far higher operational costs. Lead-acid batteries have helped in some places: Kodiak Island in Alaska was able to move to 99 percent renewable energy by using a 3MW/3 MWh lead-acid battery to reduce the need for diesel generators. In places like Alaska and Hawaii, where the electrical grid has primarily been powered by imported diesel, the cost of storage and renewables is usually cheaper—not to mention cleaner.

Not all battery storage projects have successful endings, though: the lead-acid carbon battery installed at the Koloa Solar Plant in Hawaii for the Kauai Island Utility Cooperative suffered from accelerated capacity fade.[46] Accelerated capacity fade is what happens when a battery's capacity decreases at a rate faster than expected under standard cycling and charge cycles. This capacity fade is the same problem that plagues smartphone owners: after a few years, the battery

---

45   "Battery Energy Storage System (BESS)," Golden Valley Electric Assn., accessed January 12, 2020, https://www.gvea.com/energy/bess.

46   Andy Colthorpe, "Failed Battery at Hawaii Solar Farm Part of Learning Process, Says Analyst," Energy Storage News, January 21, 2015, https://www.energy-storage.news/news/accelerated-capacity-fade-of-battery-at-hawaii-solar-farm-part-of-learning.

does not store as much energy or last as long as it did when new. This capacity fade is an expected part of using any battery, and manufacturers will usually guarantee that a battery will maintain a certain capacity after a certain number of complete charge and discharge cycles. For quality consumer batteries, these guarantees are usually 80 percent of original rated capacity after three hundred to one thousand charge cycles. The lithium-ion batteries in Apple iPhones are covered by a warranty and are considered defective if they retain less than 80 percent of original capacity after five hundred complete charge cycles.[47] The company that produced the lead-carbon electrode batteries for the Koloa Solar Plant, Extreme Power, went bankrupt due to the underperforming batteries. The plant was retired in 2018 after four years in operation.

Twelve percent of non-hydro storage facilities in 2017 were directly used to smooth or "firm" the output of renewable energy. This increases the revenue of the renewable sources by providing more reliable higher quality output, as well as allowing them to provide frequency regulation and short-term voltage control.

Electrochemical storage in the form of batteries is going to continue growing rapidly as the cost of batteries, especially lithium-ion, continues to fall over the next several years, while the revenue opportunities and value provided by storage continue to increase as intermittent renewable generation expands at an increasing rate.

---

47 "Batteries—Service and Recycling," Apple, accessed January 12, 2020, https://www.apple.com/batteries/service-and-recycling/.

Hydrogen electrolysis uses electricity to chemically split water into hydrogen and oxygen. Recombining the hydrogen and oxygen in a fuel cell—or burning the hydrogen in a turbine or piston engine—provides electricity. Currently, hydrogen is an expensive method of fuel storage because the electrolysis and fuel cells require rare and expensive catalysts like platinum. There are also substantial risks to storing large quantities of pure oxygen and hydrogen. All forms of energy can be dangerous, but hydrogen is especially challenging because the small size of hydrogen atoms allows it to squeeze through seals and containers that are airtight.

MECHANICAL STORAGE

There are three types of mechanical energy storage currently used for grid-scale storage: pumped hydro, compressed air energy storage, and flywheels. Of these, pumped hydro is the largest and cheapest, followed by compressed air energy storage and flywheels. Though it should be noted that flywheels provide high quality and more responsive power output than compressed air and pumped hydro and are more suited for high-performance applications where cost is less of an issue.

Pumped hydro is gravity-powered energy storage where water is pumped up into a holding tank or reservoir and then used to run a turbine and generator when electricity is needed. Almost 95 percent of energy storage in the United States is pumped hydro. These systems can have response times close to those of batteries and far faster than gas turbines: some pumped hydro storage facilities can go from a cold start to 100 percent output in less than ten minutes, which is far less than the one to twelve hours most thermal power plants require to reach full output. Many pumped hydro facilities are existing hydroelectric dams and are used to arbitrage the price of electricity by buying cheap electricity at night to pump water and discharging during the day when prices are high. Pumped hydro can reach 75 to 85 percent efficiency.

The downside of pumped hydro is that it cannot be built anywhere and is land-intensive where it is built. Effective pumped hydro requires two large reservoirs separated by a large height difference to produce the hydraulic head—the liquid pressure caused by the height differential and gravity—and the capacity of the pumped hydro facility is limited by the geography limitations on reservoir size. It also requires high capital costs to construct dams or reservoirs. The relative cost per MWh stored is generally lower than almost all other energy storage systems, but the total cost per system is large. The environmental impact of constructing new hydroelectric facilities can be large: ecosystems can be flooded and destroyed.

There are a few other technologies being developed that use gravity to store energy by lifting concrete blocks or rolling trains up mountains, but compared to pumped hydro, these are a drop in the bucket.

Compressed air energy storage also suffers similar issues with geographical dependence: tanks for storing large quantities of compressed air are expensive, but unused mines and retired oil wells can be extremely cheap places to store large quantities of air. Like pumped hydro, compressed air energy storage pumps a working fluid to a higher energy state—in this case, higher pressure than the atmospheric baseline—and runs that through a turbine and generator to generate electricity later.

Compressed air energy storage's primary flaw is the issue of heat: gases heat up when compressed and cool down when they decompress to a lower pressure. The noble gas law relating pressure, volume, and temperature for fixed quantity of a specific gas holds true for air and makes compressed air energy storage inefficient. When the air is compressed to store excess electricity, it heats up. Without large quantities of insulation and expensive heat exchangers, this heat is wasted. When the compressed air has cooled down and is run through a turbine to generate electricity, it cools down even further, reducing the energy content of the gas and lowering the total efficiency of the system. If all of this heating and cooling is wasted, plant efficiencies can be as low as 15 to 25 percent, which is rarely economically feasible.

Most currently operating plants in the United States are diabatic systems that use the compressed air to power gas-fired turbines. Using compressed air allows for gas turbines to operate more efficiently and shift the energy needed to compress their input air to off-peak times. This allows a gas turbine to output more energy when needed because energy that would be spent compressing air during normal operation has already been spent ahead of time, leaving extra energy to be turned into electricity.

Flywheels store energy as rotational kinetic energy by spinning weighted discs to speeds as high as 100,000 RPM.[48] Flywheels are exceptionally good at releasing small amounts of energy at extremely high output powers. By converting rotational kinetic energy into electric energy through a motor, flywheels can generate large amounts of electrical power for a short duration. This is useful for meeting unexpected changes in supply and demand like those caused by a generator failure. A flywheel can provide the energy needed for a few minutes to keep the grid stable while backup reserves are brought online. Typically, flywheels are more expensive than other forms of energy storage but provide extremely high quality and fast backup power. These qualities make them popular in data centers and other critical infrastructure where power quality is important.

In an islanded grid or backup power system, flywheels usually provide intermediate power before a battery system is used in the event of power loss. The flywheels allow for short disruptions to effectively be ignored and prevent the batteries from discharging for a disruption too short to use them. For longer power outages, a flywheel can provide energy long enough for the severity of the disruption to be determined and for the batteries to come online. For a data center, these batteries would be backed up by diesel or gas generators.

Flywheels provide an important energy storage technology in places where power quality and response speed are at a premium. Batteries can usually meet these same requirements,

---

48 "US Grid Energy Storage Factsheet," Center for Sustainable Systems, 2019, http://css.umich.edu/factsheets/us-grid-energy-storage-factsheet.

but a flywheel's response does not lose capacity with frequent use, making the total cost of storage lower in some of these situations for flywheels.

ELECTRICAL STORAGE

Purely electrical energy storage technology is not currently in use for grid-scale electrical storage due to high cost and low storage densities. There are two types of purely electrical storage that are used to store electricity and may eventually be used for grid-level storage: capacitors and superconducting magnetic storage.

Capacitors store energy in the electric fields between two conductors separated by a dielectric electrical insulator (such as vacuum, air, plastic, or ceramic among many other materials) and can release it at extremely fast speeds. Capacitors are, however, currently in use to improve the quality of the grid and to firm up the output of renewable energy projects. They also see large-scale usage in industrial applications where any disruption in power or fluctuation in power quality could be expensive or dangerous.

Capacitors also see use in areas where ultra-high discharge rates are needed. The National Ignition Fusion research facility uses capacitors to deliver a peak power of more than one terawatt (1 TW = 1000 GW = 1,000,000 MW), which is more power than the entire US electrical grid can supply. Conveniently, capacitors can store this energy and discharge much faster than they charge, leading to high power output with lower charging speeds. Capacitors are useful for grid stability and power conditioning and are popular for high-energy physics research like the National Ignition Facility.[49]

Superconducting magnetic energy storage uses superconducting materials at cryogenic temperatures to store energy. A current introduced into a superconducting coil does not experience any resistance and will continue traveling indefinitely until the material stops superconducting. This means that a superconductive loop can be used to store energy indefinitely, provided that the entire storage system is kept at extremely low temperatures.

Superconducting magnetic energy storage provides greater energy storage capacity than capacitors and high-energy flywheels but at a much greater cost. Recent advances in high-temperature superconductors are bringing down the cost of superconducting magnetic energy storage and increasing the storage capacity. Given the amount of active research in superconductivity currently (there will be at least one, if not more Nobel prizes for the scientist who finds a breakthrough that allows for low-cost high-temperature superconductors), a breakthrough in superconductive materials could allow superconducting magnetic energy storage to be built cost-effectively.

THERMAL STORAGE

Thermal storage is the storage of heat or cold to use later. Approximately half of the total energy consumption globally

---

49 "Power Conditioning," National Ignition Facility (Lawrence Livermore National Laboratory), accessed January 12, 2020, https://lasers.llnl.gov/about/how-nif-works/beamline/power-conditioning

is used for heating, so shifting that energy use in time can be more efficient. Water or other materials can be heated ahead of time and then used as a source of heating instead of electricity. Likewise, energy that will be used for cooling can be stored by freezing water and using the resulting ice as the source of cooling.

At the grid level, concentrated solar power is the primary source of thermal energy storage. Using mirrors to focus sunlight onto either water or another heat storage medium like molten sodium or other salts allows a concentrated solar power plant to concentrate the heat of the sun and use that heat to turn water into steam to generate electricity from a turbine. By increasing the amount of heated transfer fluid, energy can be stored. By pumping this heated transfer fluid into large insulated tanks, energy can be stored for long periods of time.

The Cerro Dominador Concentrated Solar Plant in Chile aims to store seventeen hours of molten salt for a 110 MW/1,870 MWh power plant. This will allow the plant, combined with another 100 MW of solar PV resources on the same site, to provide constant energy to the national grid twenty-four hours a day, seven days a week. The price of concentrated solar power is higher than solar PV, but the ability to produce energy long after the sun has set is worth a premium. The CEO of Cerro Dominador, Fernando Gonzalez, was interviewed about the costs of the project and explained that the economics worked out well: "We were awarded two [purchasing power agreements] for baseload (24×7) supply. You can't get seventeen hours of energy storage with batteries, so CSP and molten salt thermal energy storage is a good technology given the resources we have onsite."[50]

The economics and storage abilities of concentrated solar power are competitive. Other forms of thermal storage are economically competitive at smaller scales for non-electrical energy storage. There are numerous places where residential and light commercial energy storage make sense: running electric heating or cooling during off-peak times when electricity is cheap allows for cost savings and lower peak electrical consumption.

STORAGE: CONSTANTLY IMPROVING

Numerous kinds of energy storage are under development to increase the affordability and performance of energy storage. It is likely we will see a combination of incremental improvements and further breakthroughs in storage technology as existing technologies mature and reach greater economies of scale. The costs for some storage technologies like battery storage are coming down dramatically despite being young technologies.[51]

I am optimistic that we will see future breakthroughs in energy storage technology for two reasons: these technologies are extremely young, and there are a large number of

50   Andrew Burger, "Chile's 24x7 Concentrating Solar Power Plus Storage Project Is Back on Track," Solar Magazine, April 10, 2019, https://solar-magazine.com/chiles-24x7-concentrating-solar-power-plus-storage-project-is-back-on-track/

51   Lazard. 2018. "Levelized Cost of Storage Version 4.0." Lazard. https://www.lazard.com/media/450774/lazards-levelized-cost-of-storage-version-40-vfinal.pdf

extremely smart people who stand to gain fame and fortune for inventing better technology. The first experimental lithium-ion battery was built in the 1970s and only entered commercial use in 1991. The chemists Stanley Whittingham, John Goodenough, and Akira Yoshino received the 2019 Nobel Prize in chemistry for their work inventing the lithium-ion battery.[52]

Overall, large amounts of energy storage are coming online, and the costs are becoming increasingly competitive with conventional thermal generation. The global power grid will see an increasing amount of energy storage, which will help increase the flexibility of the grid and allow more renewable energy to be produced by reducing curtailment rates and increasing the profitability of renewables. But is it enough?

<hr>

52 Royal Swedish Academy of Sciences. 2019. "Press Release: The Nobel Prize in Chemistry 2019." October 9. Accessed 12 10, 2019. https://www.nobelprize.org/prizes/chemistry/2019/press-release/.

7

DISTRIBUTED FLEXIBILITY

———

The hard and stiff will be broken.
The soft and supple will prevail.

—LAO-TZU, *TAO TE CHING*

Energy flexibility is the missing link between our rapid adoption of renewable energy and a zero-emissions economy. Creating a more flexible grid will increase reliability and sustainability while decreasing costs. In addition to utility-scale energy storage, distributed small-scale generation and these distributed energy resources will provide a tremendous amount of value and help make the grid smarter, more resilient, and less carbon-intense.

DISTRIBUTED ENERGY RESOURCES

The falling cost and increasing sophistication of renewable energy and small-scale energy resources have created enthusiasm and economic activity around decentralized energy production and Distributed Energy Resources (DERs).[53] Many of these resources have existed in various forms for some electrical consumers. For example, small backup generators are in widespread use as emergency power systems for most critical infrastructure: hospitals, data centers, residential buildings' emergency safety systems, and, ironically, thermal and nuclear power plants.[54] [55]

These small generators help keep life-critical systems operational when power from the electrical grid is disrupted. Usually powered by gasoline, diesel, propane, or natural gas, these units range from a few kilowatts for residential standby power to several megawatts for large commercial backup units. Most thermal power plants like coal and gas plants need electrical power to start, which requires a connection to the electrical grid or a backup power source. These small generators are historically less efficient and

<hr>

53 David R Baker, "Battery Reality: There's Nothing Better Than Lithium-Ion Coming Soon" (Bloomberg, April 3, 2019), https://www.bloomberg.com/news/articles/2019-04-03/battery-reality-there-s-nothing-better-than-lithium-ion-coming-soon.

54 The Fukushima Daiichi nuclear accident escalated to a meltdown because the fifteen-meter tsunami destroyed the connection to the grid and flooded the standby power units, which were located ten to thirteen meters above sea level. The reactors required pumps to remove the residual heat, which were unable to operate due to the flooded standby units. Three other nearby nuclear power plants were severely damaged, with half their standby power units being washed away, but with continued electricity, they were able to manage their heat. Twelve of the thirteen backup generators were washed away or disabled at the Fukushima Daiichi Installation.

55 Robert Perkins, "Fukushima Disaster Was Preventable, New Study Finds" (University of Southern California, January 27, 2017), https://news.usc.edu/86362/fukushima-disaster-was-preventable-new-study-finds/.

more expensive when compared to larger power plants, so it is cheaper to get energy from the grid most of the time. Some sophisticated modern standby units can approach the efficiency of dedicated power plants, but these are substantially more expensive than less efficient units and are primarily used in remote areas like oil and gas wells or military bases.

While many standby units have reasonable emissions, units used only for emergency backup are held to less stringent requirements by the Environmental Protection Agency (EPA) in the United States and emit more air pollution than dedicated generators. Generators for emergency backup are also limited by the EPA to nonemergency usage of up to one hundred hours per year, including all maintenance and emergency dispatch to prevent an imminent blackout, and up to fifty hours per year of nonemergency operation. This nonemergency operation prohibits financial arrangements outside of specific agreements with appropriate local entities for grid reliability, meaning most emergency generators are never run for profit and do not usually contribute to grid reliability.

These standby power units are one of the oldest examples of electrical distributed energy resources and will continue to play a role supporting life-critical systems. However, distributed generation that uses fossil fuels is a more expensive option than centralized hydrocarbon generation. Nonemergency distributed energy resources—such as small-scale renewables, energy storage, and demand response assets— offer potentially lower costs and greater benefits than conventional hydrocarbon generation.

Renewable distributed energy resources offer reliability and financial benefits. For residential structures, solar photovoltaic, battery-based energy storage, and micro-hydro or wind installations of just a few kilowatts can be economically viable. For commercial structures, the same types of distributed generation resources are even more attractive: most commercial buildings use more energy than residential structures, have greater financial incentives and resources to reduce energy consumption, and have more tangible branding benefits from reducing carbon emissions.

Distributed energy resources have three primary benefits universal to every project where they are considered: financial benefits, reliability benefits, and environmental benefits. For most consumers and companies, the financial and reliability benefits are the most attractive part of investing in energy resources: the prospect of earning money or reducing costs makes an investment easy to evaluate, and the disruption and potentially severe costs of a hypothetical blackout are obvious to most home and business owners. Historically, when the costs of distributed generation were far higher than they are today, the environmental benefits were the primary motivating factor in distributed energy projects.

Many people will pay a premium to do the right thing environmentally, but up until around the turn of the century, most residential solar projects were financially bad investments even with tax credits and other incentives. These projects were driven by environmental motivations, just like many large corporate and commercial projects. Corporations are quite sophisticated when it comes to marketing and branding, and many distributed energy projects were part of prestige projects: it looks good to have a fancy headquarters building with solar panels on the roof or to say that a factory is carbon-neutral. These motivations have been extremely helpful in creating enough demand to finance bringing the cost of projects down to the point where economic motivations alone will drive demand.

Primarily economic motivations will drive most of the adoption of distributed energy resources over the next thirty years. The payback period for most of these assets has declined across the board as their costs have fallen and the price of energy has stayed high, making these systems pay for themselves faster. Some commercial demand response or energy storage projects can have payback periods of less than eighteen months! Even higher-cost residential energy storage is becoming cheap enough that the benefit of having storage as backup power for emergencies is being viewed as accidental to the financial payback.

Solar photovoltaic residential systems provide energy to offset the cost of energy from the electrical grid. In the US, most of these systems currently have a payback period of four to ten years depending on financial incentives, installation details, operational conditions, and system costs. These costs will continue to decrease, making them even more attractive investments. The cheapest of these systems, however, use grid-tied inverters, which do not work without the electrical grid. Unlike standalone or hybrid inverters, these grid-tied inverters require an external source to provide an AC frequency that they synchronize their output with. Standalone inverters are entirely disconnected from the grid and charge storage systems. The most expensive systems use hybrid inverters that can act as standalone inverters to charge batteries or other storage systems and synchronize with the grid to export excess energy. These hybrid systems, combined with storage to make "solar plus storage" ("Solar+"), are becoming extremely attractive in sunnier areas with high electricity prices.

To illustrate the falling costs: in 2016, one Australian man, Clayton Lyndon, spent AUD $80,000 (USD $60,000) on Tesla Powerwall storage batteries to store the energy produced from his large solar installation. Natural Solar, the company that installed the systems, estimated a four-to-six-year payback period from the savings of using stored solar energy at night. "It's a little embarrassing our household power consumption is so high, although I feel positive the financial risk will pan out and it's nice to be doing our part for the environment," Lyndon told news outlets after the installation was announced.[56] This type of solar plus storage installation—and the primarily financial motivation behind it—is becoming more common as costs decrease. The financial logic behind investments like the one Lyndon made is sound: energy assets with payback periods of four-to-five years are competitive, if not superior, when compared to investments in stocks, bonds, and other investment instruments.

---

56   Matthew Dunn, "Man Spends $80,000 to Turn His Home into Mini Battery Power Station," NewsComAu, September 14, 2016, https://www.news.com.au/technology/innovation/inventions/man-makes-mini-battery-power-station-in-his-home-after-buying-six-tesla-powerwalls/news-story/4a09a5ed7a87515a276af68b6a1296c6.

For commercial installations, storage can be especially lucrative for electrical consumers who pay a demand charge. These demand charges are based on the highest rate of power consumption, usually averaged over a fifteen-minute period, and are billed in addition to the total use of energy. Reducing this peak power usage directly reduces the amount charged, frequently by a large amount. Activities like starting large electric motors or other heavy equipment can draw huge amounts of power for brief periods. For businesses that have short periods of peak energy use that are substantially higher than their usual consumption, an investment in energy storage to cover this peak demand could have short payback periods and high internal rates of return. Lazard's 2018 levelized cost of storage report identifies global averages of 12 percent to 20 percent internal rates of return for standalone commercial storage.[57]

Commercial installations of distributed energy resources can also be lucrative if utilities offer time-of-day pricing or other pricing structures that allow for arbitrage. Time-of-day pricing differences can be arbitraged with storage that is charged during the daily off-peak period (usually overnight) and discharged during the peak pricing period to avoid paying the higher cost. This pricing difference alone is rarely enough to make a storage system economically viable but can contribute to the value of a storage installation.

Commercial storage projects of sufficiently large scale in regions with more progressive utilities can unlock additional

---

57   Lazard, 2018, Levelized Cost of Storage Version 4.0, Lazard, https://
      www.lazard.com/media/450774/lazards-levelized-cost-of-storage-ver-
      sion-40-vfinal.pdf.

revenue streams by providing emergency or auxiliary services to the local grid operator. In some areas, these revenue streams alone are enough to make a storage project viable. These commercial storage projects also allow grid operators to reduce their own investment in transmission infrastructure, as lower peak demand and increased auxiliary services increase grid stability.

Distributed energy resources also reduce the need for transmission infrastructure: a building that generates energy requires less maximum energy from the grid. The reduced utilization of transmission lines is valuable, as it allows for investments to be made in renewable generation and long-distance transmission instead of local infrastructure.

GRID DEMOCRATIZATION

Distributed energy resources and microgeneration give consumers real choice when it comes to purchasing energy. Utilities have been slow to provide sustainable energy on terms that consumers are satisfied with. Personal energy consumption has traditionally been disconnected from the cost of that energy consumption: most consumers get a bill every month and that's the end of the matter. Individual consumers are revolting at the inaction of many utilities. With the cost decreases in distributed generation, it has become competitive in many areas to produce energy locally. This grid democratization is driven by the desire for consumer choice.[58]

---

58 Shelley Welton, "Grasping for Energy Democracy," *Michigan Law Review*, 116 (2018): pp. 581-644.

True consumer choice around energy requires improvements in three areas:

- Accurate energy pricing
- Regulatory reform
- Consumer engagement

Energy pricing needs improvement so that the cost a consumer pays for energy reflects the real costs of producing and transmitting that energy. This requires two primary changes: accurate market pricing, and accounting for externalities.

Accurate energy pricing exists at the wholesale level: deregulated energy markets involve real-time prices that generally reflect the real cost of energy. If prices do not reflect the real cost, there is an opportunity for market participants to earn money by producing or consuming energy. Likewise, price signals provide a tangible incentive to change behavior or invest in new assets. These price signals generally do not exist for small consumers of electricity. Some consumers get approximations of these costs through time-of-use pricing, seasonal pricing, and peak demand charges, but these approximations only partially reflect historical grid costs.

Generating electricity from fossil fuels creates pollution. The cost of this pollution is not included in the cost of energy that consumers see. In cases where regulation puts a limit or tax on pollution, utilities and generators have to invest in emissions-control solutions to reduce pollution and build the cost of that equipment into their prices. For carbon-dioxide emissions, the global costs do not get included in prices paid by consumers. Not pricing these externalities into the cost of energy creates a market distortion that makes energy from carbon sources artificially cheap. Fixing this pricing error would allow consumers to make more informed decisions that accurately reflect total costs. The cheapest energy source that satisfies requirements is the correct choice, but only if the sticker price accurately reflects the total costs.

Regulatory reform is needed to allow customers to produce their own energy. Luckily, these reforms are underway in many parts of the United States. Traditionally, utilities could set rates at a level just high enough to recoup investment and a fixed profit margin. This pricing structure incentivized utilities to invest more in the grid so that they earn more profit. If utility customers produce their own energy, vertically integrated utilities under the old model stand to earn less money. These same utilities tend to drag their feet when asked to accept distributed energy. Deregulation has broken up many of these entities so that generation and transmission are not owned by the same entity. Deregulation has reduced this issue, but there is still room for improvement.

We also need consumer engagement and education to enable full consumer choice and grid democratization. Consumers need to know that they can make their own choices about energy, what those choices are, and how they can choose. The choices that consumers make determine the sustainability, reliability, and affordability of the grid, so education is needed to help them make informed choices that are optimal for the consumer and the overall power grid.

Better yet, let consumers choose to make these decisions automatically. Manually choosing how and when to consume energy is too time-consuming to reasonably expect most of us to do it. Turning on the dishwasher or air conditioning unit should not require a cost-benefit analysis each time it is done. Automated decision-making allows consumers to get most out of a democratized grid without constantly thinking about it. A well-designed and -managed set of options for consumers can reduce costs and carbon emissions for consumers and utilities alike.

8

DEMAND RESPONSE

——

The second part of a distributed and flexible electric grid is being responsive to demand. Balancing supply and demand is traditionally achieved by increasing supply and turning on additional generators. But what if grid operators could reduce demand instead?

Demand response technologies allow grid operators and utilities to reduce demand. These technologies and programs allow consumers and businesses to give control of appliances and machinery to utilities, who can shut off or reduce the load from that device. If a utility can reduce demand from enough devices, the total reduction in demand can be sufficient to avoid the need to dispatch peaking plants or start mandatory load shedding. With enough electrical load committed to a demand response program, utilities can defer costly investments in new transmission or generation.

RESIDENTIAL DEMAND RESPONSE
Many utilities in the United States and around the world also have pricing structures designed to reduce peak demand

and make it easier and cheaper for utilities to supply electricity and keep the grid operating reliably. Typically, these are time-of-day prices and demand charges based on peak demand. For the typical residential consumer, however, these pricing structures either do not apply or are insufficiently motivational. An increased cost of $0.05 per kilowatt-hour during peak hours is not enough to discourage most residential customers from turning on the air conditioning when the additional cost adds up to a few cents.

Automatic schemes are more effective at encouraging changes in consumer behavior.

The classic example of a demand response program is air conditioning. Many utilities have programs where residential homeowners can opt-in to a program where the utility can take control of the residence's air conditioning unit on hot days. The utility is able to turn down the air conditioning unit or turn it off entirely, which reduces load by about three to five kilowatts for a typical air conditioning unit in the United States. If a utility can get thousands of customers to participate, the amount of demand that can be reduced is comparable to a decent-sized power plant. Customers are usually compensated for their participation, making demand response programs a win-win: customers get cheaper electricity in exchange for sweating a little more on hot days, and utilities can avoid the cost of dispatching peaking generators or building new transmission and generation assets.

My utility, Pepco, has a clever advertising scheme to label peak demand days as "Peak Savings Days." It offers discounts to customers who enroll to reduce demand during those days. Other utilities have similar programs that attempt to incentivize and modify consumer behavior to varying effects. Pepco's Energy Wise Reward program is an example of a successful residential demand response program.

Pepco has enrolled over 360,000 customers in Maryland in its demand response program, giving Pepco 300 megawatts of demand to turn off on hot days.[59] Customers receive billing credits by allowing Pepco to install a smart thermostat that can control a home's air conditioning unit. For each month the program is running, June through October, participating customers receive a credit in exchange for allowing Pepco to remotely reduce the time the air conditioning unit's compressor runs during peak demand days. During these "Peak Savings Days," customers who opted into the 50 percent cycling program will see their air conditioner run 50 percent of the time it would have normally during the peak period. Customers on the 100 percent plan have their air conditioning unit's compressor turn off entirely during the typical three-to-six-hour long conservation period. This program allows Pepco to defer investment in new peaking resources and transmission upgrades and passes some of the savings back to customers.

Historically, there has been minimal to no real-time communication between electrical supply and demand. Power plants can measure aggregate demand by seeing how much power they have to generate to maintain grid voltage and frequency,

---

59   Robert Walton, "Pepco Enrolls Half of Eligible Comverge Demand Response Customers," Utility Dive, December 23, 2014, https://www. utilitydive.com/news/pepco-enrolls-half-of-eligible-comverge-demand-response-customers/346805/.

and consumers can measure the quality of the electricity they're receiving—or for residential and most commercial consumers, whether they are receiving electricity—but there has not been much real-time communication between them. Meters measure consumption and bills are sent out at the end of the billing period, but, with the exception of the largest industrial consumers of electricity, most consumers never get any sense of how the electrical grid is operating. This is changing, and now residential consumers, and their networked devices, can see how much energy they are using in real-time, where that energy is coming from, and how much they are spending on it.

Demand response at the residential level allows utilities to make the grid more flexible, which reduces overall system costs and the cost of electricity for residential consumers.

Industrial Demand Response

Large industrial consumers of electricity receive low prices on wholesale electricity, usually in exchange for consuming a constant amount of electricity and avoiding large increases in consumption. These large consumers are incentivized to manage their energy demand—to specifically keep their demand flat through peak demand charges and pricing structures that make high-peak electricity consumption prohibitively expensive. Some of these customers, especially those in industries like smelting where electrical consumption is massive but disruptions are less costly, may agree to voluntarily reduce consumption to almost zero in the event of grid disruption. In South Australia, for example, after the 2016 blackouts, the Australian Energy Market Operator secured contracts with industrial consumers for almost 850 megawatts of demand response for use in emergencies.60

Many industrial consumers have historically been poorly situated to use demand response: suddenly turning off equipment can be disruptive at best, catastrophic at worse. As discussed in the previous chapter, the falling cost of energy storage and backup generation has caused a growing share of businesses to invest in equipment that allows them to generate their own energy in emergencies, or at least disconnect from the grid gracefully. This is still disruptive to the institutions who are impacted but is better than the alternatives: blackouts.

Flexible demand that a utility can influence or fully control provides a powerful tool in ensuring grid stability and reducing total costs. When talking about controlling demand, it is important to make explicit that this is a conversation about voluntary demand response. Utilities and grid operators already have the ability to introduce rolling blackouts or disconnect specific large consumers to make sure that the grid continues running. Blackouts and outages are hugely disruptive but are preferable to total grid failure. While rolling blackouts and wide-scale outages are not generally considered graceful degradation, they are preferable to experiencing a total blackout and having to go through a blackstart: starting the entire grid from a full-stop is hazardous, slow, and technically complicated. Load reduction

---

60　Nick Harmsen, "How We Got through Summer Without Load-Shedding Blackouts," ABC News, May 23, 2018, https://www.abc.net.au/news/2018-05-23/no-load-shedding-over-hot-summer/9792802.

in the form of demand response is a powerful tool to make the grid more flexible.

VEHICLE DEMAND RESPONSE

Electric vehicles are a growing part of the energy equation that utilities will need to plan for. Widespread adoption of electric vehicles will lead to a large increase in residential electricity demand as the energy that came from gasoline will now need to be provided by the grid. Projections from Bloomberg's New Energy Finance forecast that the electrical consumption of electric vehicles in the United States will rise from 6 terawatt-hours in 2018 to 1,800 terawatt-hours by 2040, which would make up more than 40 percent of the total electrical demand of the current US grid.[61] This massive increase in demand will require investment in infrastructure but will also provide substantial benefits.

Some of this benefit may come from vehicle-to-grid applications where electric vehicles equipped with bidirectional chargers actively put power into the grid, but this is unlikely to become the primary benefit of electric vehicles to the grid because of concerns about battery degradation. As discussed earlier, electrochemical batteries, like those found in electric vehicles, lose capacity with every charge cycle.[62] Given most consumers' anxiety around range, an electric vehicle's owner

61   Steve Hanley, "Vehicle to Grid Plan Pays Off for Electric Car Drivers in Europe," enrg.io, June 13, 2019, https://enrg.io/vehicle-grid-plan-pays-off-electric-car-drivers-europe.

62   "Electric Vehicle-To-Grid Technology Gears Up for the Mass Market (#CleanTechnica Interview)," CleanTechnica, July 19, 2019, https://cleantechnica.com/2019/01/26/electric-vehicle-to-grid-technology-gears-up-for-the-mass-market-cleantechnica-interview.

likely needs additional compensation to be convinced to let their vehicle feed power into the grid. If using cars as portable energy storage is undesirable, then why not use them for demand response?

If the grid is allowed to manage large portions of this demand flexibly, it could reduce total costs by adjusting demand based on forecast renewable energy production and other factors. If an electric car is plugged in at 6:00 p.m. and not used again until 8:00 a.m. the next day, the charging could happen anytime overnight.

Just the information of when the vehicles charge and what that demand looks like is valuable to utilities: the company Fleetcarma has a pilot with New York's Con Edison utility for participating electric vehicle users to receive up to $650 in compensation for their charging data and behavioral modifications to shift charging to off-peak times.[63] If a utility has access to enough local electric vehicle data, they can build a model to predict what demand will be three to twenty-four hours in advance. If given access to location or battery data, a utility could compare the current activity of electric vehicles to previous activity and forecast when those vehicles will charge and how much demand they'll generate. This type of insight into demand will be especially valuable as transportation continues to electrify and energy from gasoline and diesel is replaced by electrical energy—hopefully, from renewable sources.

---

63   "SmartCharge New York," FleetCarma, accessed January 12, 2020, https://www.fleetcarma.com/smartchargenewyork.

Electric vehicles will be one of the most important sources of demand response in the electrical grid of the future, but residential and commercial applications will also be important, especially for shifting peak loads around to be more flexible. Load shifting—when an electrical load is shifted from a period of peak demand to an off-peak period—results in flatter demand. That in turn allows that demand to be supplied at a lower price in most circumstances.[64]

Real-time pricing already occurs for wholesale electricity. Passing some of that information back to the end consumer can incentivize behavior modification and reduce load when energy supplies are tight. Smart meters in residential settings can communicate with connected appliances and vehicles and tell them to reduce or delay consumption.

DEMAND RESPONSE BENEFITS

Demand response gives utilities a great tool to reduce stress on the grid and on power plants. With smarter consumption of electricity, the sustainability, reliability, stability, and cost of the grid can be improved. As we've discussed in previous chapters, managing peak demand and ramping to daily peaks are challenging and expensive.

The ideal load for a conventional thermal plant or nuclear plant is constant: generators and turbines are generally built for optimal performance within a relatively tight range of

---

64   Giles Parkinson and Bridie Schmidt, "Electric Cars Can Smooth Grid and Reduce Energy Prices," The Driven, April 10, 2019, https://the-driven.io/2019/04/09/electric-cars-can-smooth-grid-and-reduce-energy-prices-report-says/.

operating conditions. Operation outside of these parameters is acceptable without risking damage to the plant, but efficiency is reduced, which lowers the amount of profit possible through either decreased revenue (less electricity being produced) or higher costs (more fuel consumed). In some cases, operating a generator at high levels of output can increase the amount of maintenance required: moving parts forced to move faster encounter greater wear and tear, and conventional bearings will have to be replaced more often. In almost all cases, operating a plant at the target capacity is the lowest cost and most efficient option.

Demand response thinking and technology has been around for a long time. However, only in the last decade has the cost of networking and computing fallen so much that it is now more expensive to configure a device than to add computing power to that device in the first place. Data analysis has gotten faster and more sophisticated as computers and storage have gotten cheaper. Production systems are substantially more powerful thanks to advances in algorithms and machine-learning prediction systems. The limiting factors for residential demand response technology in new appliances are regulation, incentive structuring, privacy, and security. Many appliances are becoming smart by default, and most of the features needed for them to respond to demand response signals could be added through software updates.

Demand response programs allow utilities to aggregate small energy savings into massive grid-level reductions. This aggregation provides more value than the sum of the total reductions: by knowing in advance how much demand response can be dispatched, utilities can make better long-term plans in addition to the short-term savings. Aggregating small energy resources provides great value when utilities do it. Why not allow private companies and individuals to voluntarily aggregate their own energy resources and get compensated for the value they provide?

9

VIRTUAL POWER PLANTS

—

Although the virtual power plant is in its early days, it is already demonstrating how it can provide the network support traditionally performed by large conventional generators.

—DAN VAN HOLST PELLEKAAN, MINISTER FOR
ENERGY AND MINING, SOUTH AUSTRALIA

Virtual power plants are groups of networked distributed energy resources that can be dispatched like a conventional power plant. These can be created by utilities like the demand response programs discussed in the previous chapter or assembled by private companies and compete on wholesale power markets.

Virtual power plants can provide three primary benefits: increasing the value of distributed energy storage, decreasing the stress caused by behind-the-meter distributed generation, and lowering the cost of charging electric vehicles. These benefits come from increased flexibility in when energy is produced or consumed and/or more detailed insight into distributed energy resource assets and behavior that allow grid operators to make better decisions.

AGGREGATING DISTRIBUTED STORAGE

Virtual power plants can be used to make distributed energy storage more profitable, while decreasing the overall cost of electricity. A virtual power plant made from homes that are equipped with energy storage is like a demand response system on steroids that can respond to market prices.

Smart grids integrating distributed storage with traditional generation can reduce the need for peaking plants, allowing utilities to reduce overall costs and compensate residential energy storage owners. By consolidating resources into virtual power plants that bid in electricity spot markets, individual energy storage owners can earn more profit than storing cheaper energy to avoid peak time-of-use surcharges. Greater profits on residential energy storage systems incentivize investment and adoption, yielding additional benefits to the grid.

In Australia, AGL is installing 11.6 MWh of residential batteries to form a virtual power plant that can be dispatched by the utility to meet peak demand.[65] When not dispatched, the batteries will charge from excess solar capacity and offset the homeowners' consumption. Tesla and Green Mountain Power are blending utility-owned industrial energy storage with shared-ownership residential batteries to form a 10 MW

---

65   "AGL Virtual Power Plant—Australian Renewable Energy Agency (ARENA)," Australian Renewable Energy Agency, accessed January 12, 2020, https://arena.gov.au/projects/agl-virtual-power-plant.

virtual power plant that will act as a peaking plant for GMP and backup power source for residents.[66] New York's Con Edison utility was running a 2 MW pilot project to test the feasibility of selling stored energy to the competitive market through a virtual power plant and believes that similar virtual power plants could generate returns on investment of 8 percent by 2021.[67]

Distributed energy storage will be adopted when it is profitable, necessary for grid stability, or required as backup. For behind-the-meter energy storage to be profitable, it must result in greater overall savings or income than the cost of installation. For markets with a peak demand or time-of-use surcharge to consumers, savings occur when energy storage is used for arbitrage between peak demand pricing and off-peak pricing. Purchasing energy during off-peak hours is cheaper than purchasing that energy during peak hours, allowing for savings to be realized. In the US, off-peak energy can be more than 25 percent cheaper from utilities that offer time-varying rates. For most consumers, this peak surcharge differential would result in small savings that do not currently make it profitable to install energy storage without another source of revenue.

The Tesla Powerwall 2.0 comes with a ten-year warranty at a cost of $6,700 for a 14 KWh system. Installed in Hawaii to

---

66 "GMP Launches New Comprehensive Energy Home Solution from Tesla to Lower Costs for Customers," Green Mountain Power, accessed January 12, 2020, https://greenmountainpower.com/news/gmp-launches-new-comprehensive-energy-home-solution-tesla-lower-costs-customers/.

67 Con Edison, 2017, "REV Demonstration Project: Clean Virtual Power Plant 2016 Q4 Quarterly Progress Report."

take advantage of the $0.085 peak time of day surcharge, the system could pay for itself in a little over fifteen years. Typical installation fees and inefficiencies result in a likely payback period of nearly twenty years at current prices. There is no guarantee that the system will last the entire payback period, making it a risky investment without the added benefit of having a backup source of electricity. Without additional value beyond arbitraging time-of-day pricing, this would be unattractive because of the risk of system failure before the investment has broken even. Home energy storage adoption will not be driven by profit motives if the payback period is longer than the expected lifetime.

Costs for lithium-ion-based energy storage are projected to fall to less than $200/KWh by 2020.[68] A 10 KWh home battery installed in 2020 will have a payback period of nearly eleven years with a time-of-day surcharge of $0.05/KWh, assuming the battery is utilized fully to offset peak demand with stored off-peak energy. This payback period of eleven years is unattractive to most consumers, due to the expected lifespan of storage systems to be around ten years in most cases. The attractiveness is highly dependent on regulatory actions, subsidies, and utility policy, as a $200/KWh storage system would have an expected payback period of 7.2 years under Hawaii Electric's time-of-use rates.

Coordinating behind-the-meter energy storage to form a virtual power plant and bid in electricity spot markets as a

---

68 "The New Economics of Energy Storage," McKinsey & Company, accessed January 12, 2020, https://www.mckinsey.com/business-functions/sustainability/our-insights/the-new-economics-of-energy-storage.

peaking plant would allow for a greater return on investment. By acting as a peaking plant, the distributed energy storage would be more effectively utilized overall and the storage owners would earn a profit on the stored energy greater than their savings would be from consuming that energy themselves. These storage systems would primarily be used to offset personal demand, but the rare occasion when they were successfully used as a virtual power plant could provide meaningful improvements in the payback period.

A $2,000 10 KWh home energy storage system with a $0.05/KWh peak surcharge has a payback period of 10.9 years. If this system was integrated into a virtual power plant that made bids on the electricity spot market for extremely lucrative peaking, the stored energy would be sold to the utility when the bid was successful. If the virtual power plant's bid was successful frequently enough to result in the average profit increasing by a single cent to $0.06/KWh, that would result in a 16.6 percent reduction in payback period. Spot prices for peak generation are hundreds or thousands of times more expensive than baseload generation due to the need for the electrical grid to always be balanced. If the virtual power plant could replace gas peaking plants, the payback period would improve by 10.3 percent to 14.3 percent at current levelized costs.[69] Undercutting the levelized cost of gas peaking plants by 20 percent to increase the competitiveness of the virtual power plant would still result in payback period reductions of between 7.6 percent and 11.0 percent: more than a year faster at best. These savings are

---

69   Lazard, 2016, "Levelized Cost of Energy Analysis Version 10."

conservative, as battery storage can ramp up instantaneously, unlike conventional peaking plants.

Island grids that rely on expensive diesel peaking plants could be even better for distributed storage based virtual power plants. Diesel peaking plants are far more expensive than gas peaking plants, so the payback period for a $200/KWh battery system operating as part of a virtual power plant could be reduced by 19 percent to under six years in Hawaii without any subsidies. This would be an attractive investment, especially as part of a solar installation that could charge the storage system for reduced variable costs.

The value of coordinating distributed energy storage resources is dependent on the wholesale electricity markets for specific regions. These markets must be competitive and allow independent generators for a virtual power plant to operate. The value of selling stored energy back into the grid during peak demand depends on how expensive traditional peaking generation is. In regions where load following hydro provides peaking, the value of a distributed storage virtual power plant is less than when the peaking competition is primarily inefficient and expensive gas turbines. High levels of intermittent renewable market penetration also improve the attractiveness of energy storage by providing opportunities for cheap or free energy. Areas like Hawaii and Germany have sufficient renewable market share that days occur when significant percentages of solar and wind generation can be curtailed: perfectly good energy goes unused because there is no immediate demand and a reserve of baseload generation is required. Virtual power plants made from distributed storage that is connected to wholesale energy markets could readily accept excess renewable capacity while simultaneously providing a rapid response reserve.

Time-varying pricing is a critical factor for investment in energy storage. Without the backup possibility of saving money by consuming stored electricity during peak periods when peaking capacity was not needed, the payback of a storage system is much less certain. Peaking generation utilization factors are always poor but are sometimes incredibly poor. Without time-of-day or real-time pricing that allowed for arbitrage between cheap and expensive power from a utility, distributed energy storage only provides backup power.

Forming virtual power plants from independent residential storage systems could increase the profitability of those systems in regions with favorable regulation and market landscapes. This additional profitably would increase investment in home energy storage, which would be of great benefit to local electrical grids. Peaking plant owners may lose out as their revenues are taken by the cheaper virtual power plant peaking, but overall, costs for the electrical grid and for end consumers will decrease with additional storage in place. Given current deployments with distributed and large-scale energy storage, the benefits of installing energy storage are already greater than the costs in most regions and will be profitable to implement in many areas if storage costs continue decreasing. The rise of solar-plus-storage installations creates the opportunity to aggregate substantial amounts of behind-the-meter storage into virtual power plants that can create more value for asset owners and the grid overall.

INSIGHT INTO BEHIND-THE-METER GENERATION

Virtual power plants can provide insight into behind-the-meter generation. Historically, grid operators have forecast demand and dispatched generation, but now with the increasing democratization of the grid, the challenging part is forecasting distributed generation. Aggregating that generation into a virtual power plant gives utilities insight that they would not have otherwise.

Virtual power plants can be made of any resources that can be controlled over the internet. Solar PV with a networked smart meter could be used to make a virtual power plant. Coordinating distributed generation also creates information about generation capacity, which allows market participants to make better decisions. An example of this information creation is the coordination of solar PV resources into a virtual power plant. Fifty MW of distributed solar PV capacity installed behind the meter will reduce consumption by 50 MW. Turning those resources into a 50 MW virtual power plant will not change supply or demand but will inform the utility that the 50 MW reduction in demand is because of the solar PV capacity. This information allows the utility to make more accurate forecasting so that they'll know to expect a 50 MW increase in demand on cloudy days.

ELECTRIC VEHICLE CHARGING

Many electric vehicles have the ability for smart charging. This allows an owner to set charging times and take advantage of time-of-day pricing. These programs are effective at reducing the individual cost to an electric vehicle's owner, but they do not unlock the flexibility that vehicle demand can provide: by aggregating electric vehicle charging demand into a virtual power plant, grid operators can dispatch that aggregate demand to help balance the grid while dispatching the cheapest and most environmentally friendly resources.

If enough electric vehicles were set to charge at a certain time, their aggregate demand would be easy to use as a tool by having the chargers bid to reduce demand in the wholesale energy markets. That's eMotorWerks' strategy in California, where they have aggregated more than ten thousand electric car chargers to monetize California ISO's proxy demand resource market.[70] By shifting charging schedules so vehicles charge a little slower or a little later, the aggregate demand can be used as if it was a 30 MW/70 MWh virtual battery.[71] By aggregating electric vehicle demand into a virtual power plant, everyone wins: vehicle owners can save money by charging a little later, utilities can redirect investment toward more clean energy, carbon emissions can be reduced by integrating more renewables into the grid, and electrical prices can decrease.

This will be true wherever there are increasing amounts of intermittent renewable energy resources and increasing electrification of transportation. Daniel Hilson, CEO of the electric vehicle consulting group Evenergi, researched this

---

70 Julian Spector, "EMotorWerks Is Using Its Network of 10,000 EV Chargers to Bid Into Wholesale Markets" (Greentech Media, September 25, 2018), https://www.greentechmedia.com/articles/read/emotorwerks-wholesale-markets-ev-charger-network#gs.l4r5rj.

71 Peter Maloney, "EMotorWerks Provides CAISO with 30 MW of DR through Smart EV Charging," Utility Dive, September 12, 2018, https://www.utilitydive.com/news/emotorwerks-provides-caiso-with-30-mw-of-dr-through-smart-ev-charging/532110.

matter for the South Australian government and came to the conclusion that electric vehicles could be a great asset to the grid: "By encouraging EV charging at times when there is surplus energy and limiting the amount of charging during times of peak demand, we can potentially create a more efficient, balanced, and flexible grid."

HYBRID VIRTUAL POWER PLANTS

Multiple types of resources could be combined into a virtual power plant. A residential home with a solar installation, battery energy storage, electric vehicle, and smart thermostat could participate in a virtual power plant and use some or all of those resources to reduce or increase demand based on market prices. This adds a level of complexity but allows larger virtual power plants, which would have the ability to participate more in wholesale energy markets.

By aggregating distributed energy resources through the internet to form virtual power plants, the grid can become more flexible, which increases sustainability, reliability, and affordability.

10

CRYPTO AND BLOCKCHAIN

———

If we look at the life cycle of technologies, we see an early period of over-enthusiasm, then a 'bust' when disillusionment sets in, followed by the real revolution.

—RAY KURZWEIL

Many people hear "virtual power plant" and think of cryptocurrency and blockchain. Is blockchain the best technology to connect distributed storage and keep track of energy for flexible systems? This chapter will explore blockchain and look at how it is inferior to conventional distributed system design but might get used anyway because of the hype.

THE BLOCKCHAIN

What is blockchain and why should we care? Blockchain is a family of digital networking and storage technologies that have taken the world by storm since the cryptocurrency

Bitcoin was launched in 2008 and grew to implausibly high prices. Blockchain kicked off a huge boom in distributed systems research and development and has created real opportunities to build more secure distributed systems.

Blockchain is a change-resistant distributed ledger technology that allows information to be securely stored. For a typical blockchain ledger, the data is stored in a digital ledger on multiple computers. This digital ledger is a table that contains a row for each change. These entries are never deleted, so the ledger contains a record of all changes and transactions that occur. This means that a properly configured blockchain contains a record of all changes and cannot be modified without every copy of the blockchain being updated to show that the change occurred.

These distributed blockchains are updated by consensus algorithms. These voting algorithms allow a block of updates to be agreed on by either a majority of members or those who are working the hardest to keep the ledger updated. These different types of consensus algorithms are referred to as proof of stake and proof of work.

Proof of stake consensus algorithms are typically used by corporate blockchain systems where computing overhead must remain low and weight the consensus voting by how large a stake each voter has in the system or outcome. Proof of work requires that the system must do some wasted work to vote. In the case of Bitcoin, a proof of work blockchain, consensus is reached by computers attempting to find the random number that will make a block of proposed transactions return the correct result for a cryptographic hash function. Proof of work can be extremely energy-intensive, which makes it expensive and environmentally friendly.

These blockchains can also be permissioned or permissionless. A permissionless blockchain is a public blockchain where anyone can attempt to add transactions and updates.[72] For permissionless proof of work blockchains like Bitcoin and many cryptocurrencies, new blocks with updates and transactions can be proposed by anyone, but to be accepted, they must be the first to find the correct result to a cryptographic hash function, which requires guessing an increasingly difficult-to-guess number. Bitcoin, Etherium, and most other cryptocurrencies reward the first person to mine a block with currency. People submitting transactions to a public list of transactions to be processed can add a transaction fee that is added to a miner's reward if that transaction is in the mined block.

For permissioned blockchains, only those nodes and computer systems that have permission can vote on updates and new blocks. Some critics of permissioned blockchains argue that because they are not public and distributed to an arbitrary number of people, they are not really authentic blockchains, but outside of cryptocurrency, most corporate blockchains are permissioned. Indeed, most corporate blockchains are shared ledgers, which have security, energy, and performance advantages over cryptocurrency-style blockchains. For example, IBM's Hyperledger Fabric Blockchain Solution is actually just a distributed write-only database,

---

72   "What Is Blockchain Technology?" CoinDesk, accessed December 10, 2019, https://www.coindesk.com/information/what-is-the-difference-between-open-and-permissioned-blockchains.

which provides a fantastic solution to companies that want blockchain solutions: distributed secure systems without the disadvantages of true blockchains.

THE BENEFITS

What are the benefits of using a blockchain-based system for dispatching and tracking energy storage and flexible resources?

Dr. Mihaela Ulieru, the president of the IMPACT Institute for the Digital Economy, a global agenda council advisor to the World Economic Forum at Davos, and an advisor to Bitlumens, among numerous other positions, and an expert and advocate of blockchain technology, said, "When it comes to energy, the blockchain is enabling economic models—tokenomics—which are not possible without decentralization."[73] These blockchain token-based reward systems can be used to incentivize behavior and provide compensation to participants for providing or using energy at particular times and in specific ways. Bitlumens, for example, provides a novel cryptocurrency-based reward system for solar energy development and lighting projects where participants in rural areas are rewarded with credit and digital tokens for engaging in environmentally friendly behaviors and can use the tokens to pay for electricity. "The point is the new economics that are enabled."

More important for energy than the blockchain technology itself—according to Dr. Ulieru—is the new corporate

---

73   Dr. Mihaela Ulieru, Interview, February 22, 2019.

willingness to look at how distributed computer systems can communicate with each other to increase economic value: "There is the economy of devices, which we would do with the internet of things. How do we do that? Devices talk to each other now. They can talk to each other and say 'Well, my battery is getting low,' 'Okay, I have more battery than you, okay, I'll disconnect and run on battery so you can plug in.'" This communication between a network of smart devices that can store energy will be extremely useful. If an electrical utility can get updates on the distributed storage capacity and potential demand in real time, they can dispatch energy more efficiently, which would lead to lower total costs. "There's the issue of governance. Algorithmic governance. With algorithmic governance, you can do that for energy."

The electrical grid of the future will be smart, distributed, and decentralized. Blockchain technologies could be a part of that, but modern high-performance distributed systems will be a better solution for most energy projects and distributed energy resources. There are valuable technological developments and innovations in the crypto space that should be leveraged to improve the energy grid, but the most useful element of blockchain for the energy space will actually be the innovation and development around blockchain, not the technology itself. The corporate world is now investing heavily in distributed systems and blockchain solutions, but the most important thing is that investment, not the technology.

11

COSTS

———

*There is no guarantee that the investment at the scale needed
will be made in a timely way, or that government policies will
be wisely implemented. Certainly, lead times can be long, and
costs will have to evolve.*

—DANIEL YERGIN, *THE QUEST*

The biggest obstacle currently facing a more flexible power
grid is cost. Modernizing grid infrastructure is expensive,
and a huge amount of investment is needed to reduce planetary carbon emissions to at least zero. The amount of action
required to limit global warming to two degrees Celsius—let
alone 1.5 degrees—is staggering. The high cost of action is
one of the biggest obstacles to limiting global warming to
1.5 degrees.

There are four strong reasons why the cost of modernizing the electrical grid and investing in energy technology
is not just the morally right thing to do but a worthwhile
investment. The first is that the cost of inaction is higher
than the cost of action. Second, huge amounts of electrical

infrastructure need to be replaced anyway, and replacing it with environmentally friendly renewable resources would stimulate economic activity. Third, the cost of renewables and flexible grid technologies have come down so much in cost that the cost is no longer prohibitive. And fourth, if the costs of the health and climate impact of fossil fuel combustion are accounted for, renewable and storage is a cheaper combination.

THE COST OF INACTION

The cost of actions to reduce carbon emissions are high, but the cost of inaction will be far greater. The Intergovernmental Panel on Climate Change estimates that at least $2.4 trillion in investment is required between 2016 and 2035 to limit warming to 1.5 degrees.[74] This sum needs to come from private finance and government to replace existing assets and build new energy resources to meet any growth in demand.

The costs of inaction may be higher, but we are not forced to pay for inaction upfront. The United States Government Accountability Office estimates that from 2003 to 2013, extreme weather events and fires have cost the United States government $350 billion.[75] This number is forecast to increase as the frequency of extreme weather events and volatile unpredictable climate events increase.

---

74 "No More Excuses: Financing 1.5C," Climate KIC, accessed January 12, 2020, https://www.climate-kic.org/news/no-more-excuses-financ-ing-1-5c/.

75 "Climate Change: Information on Potential Economic Effects Could Help Guide Federal Efforts to Reduce Fiscal Exposure," US Government Accountability Office (US GAO), October 24, 2017, https://www.gao.gov/products/GAO-17-720.

More comprehensive estimates put the total cost of climate change increased weather events and health effects from fossil fuel consumption at $240 billion per year in the United States alone, potentially rising to $360 billion per year by 2030.[76] Natural disasters like Hurricane Katrina and the Californian droughts have been extraordinarily costly in human and economic impact in the United States, and natural disasters are not just a problem for the United States and other wealthy nations.

The human impact and relative economic impact of climate change will fall disproportionately on the world's developing countries. The two billion least well-off humans in Africa, India, and Asia are simultaneously the most susceptible to the increasing frequency of extreme weather events and the least well equipped to be resilient in the face of these increasingly likely adverse weather events.[77] The governments of these regions are also some of the least stable globally—and in an era of political instability and turmoil, that is a strong statement—which increases the risk of mass migration, climate refugees, humans rights abuses, and military conflict.

Already the planet has seen mass migration and conflict caused by economic factors triggered by natural disasters. The Syrian Civil War and the Arab Spring were in large part triggered by environmental changes, which were likely

<hr>

76   "The Economic Case for Climate Action in the United States," Universal Ecological Fund, accessed January 12, 2020, https://feu-us.org/case-for-climate-action-us.

77   Climate Vulnerable Forum, 2016, "Pursuing the 1.5C Limit: Benefits & Opportunities," Low Carbon Monitor.

caused or exacerbated by climate change.[78] Analysis of tree rings and their moisture history—one of the best proxies for total precipitation and available water—suggests that the period of 1998–2012 was the driest recorded period in Syria and the Levant area in the past nine hundred years! Some climate modeling suggests that climate change made Syria two to three times more likely to experience drought. The drought that did occur caused numerous young people to leave agricultural regions to search for economic opportunity in the already overcrowded cities. Overcrowding, high unemployment, justified political grievances against a repressive regime, and religious strife—all the classic ingredients of a civil war—did the rest. The counterfactual, that the civil war would not have happened if there had been no drought, is impossible to prove. However, estimates of the number of Syrians displaced or reduced to severe poverty in the eighteen months before the uprising began range from eight hundred thousand to three million, or almost 5 to 15 percent of the population, which seems like the type of destabilizing event that could lead to conflict.

The economic and human costs of inaction are unacceptably high. A modernized and flexible electrical grid will not mitigate all climate change, but it is a step in the right direction.

---

78 Center for Climate and Security, 2017, "The Climate Factor in Syrian Instability," September 8, accessed December 10, 2019, https://climate-andsecurity.org/2017/09/08/the-climate-factor-in-syrian-instability-a-conversation-worth-continuing/.

THE GRID NEEDS INVESTMENT ANYWAY

The electrical grid in the United States is sorely in need of investment anyway. Just looking at generation alone, in the United States, 500 GW of thermal generation is expected to retire by 2030. Replacing this generation is necessary to provide enough supply to meet demand and is likely to cost $500 billion to $1 trillion to replace. Replacing it entirely with gas turbines would cost some $500 billion in capital expenditures, and require another $400–500 billion in operational and fuel costs over the lifespans of the plants. Replacing this capacity with a mixture of renewables and storage would cost between 40 percent and 106 percent of the cost of building and operating that same 500 GW of gas turbines.[79] Sixty percent cheaper is a good deal. Likewise, investment in transmission is needed to reduce congestion and replace aging power lines.

The amount of economic activity that would need to occur to reach near-zero carbon emissions would be a great benefit to the countries that engaged in it. Political rhetoric around a Green New Deal is still fierce, but renewable energy technology is already creating jobs in the United States and around the world. In the United States, employment in the clean energy sector is growing by 3.6 percent annually and even faster in Texas and California.[80] Given that concerns about sustaining economic growth while

---

79 Rocky Mountain Institute, 2018, "The Economics of Clean Energy Portfolios," Rocky Mountain Institute.

80 *San Antonio Business Journal, "Report Shows Texas 2nd in Nation for Clean Energy Jobs," March 14, accessed December 10, 2019, https://www. bizjournals.com/sanantonio/news/2019/03/14/report-shows-texas-2nd-in-nation-for-clean-energy.html.*

limiting greenhouse gas emissions are so large in the debates around sustainable development, the conclusions should be that any kind of energy technology is good for growth in the short term.

RENEWABLES ARE AFFORDABLE

The costs of renewable energy resources have come down so much that they are now competitive with fossil fuel electrical generation, and the cost of renewables with energy storage and a flexible grid is dropping quickly and is already competitive in some areas. If the $260 billion used to subsidize fossil fuel exploration and products globally was instead used to subsidize the cleaner and smarter use of renewable energy, it would be the obvious choice.

Making the grid flexible enough to accommodate 100 percent renewable energy will require additional investments beyond the generation itself, but even with the extra investment, renewables are still near parity with conventional energy sources. Much of this investment makes the grid more resilient and reliable.

In the long term, however, not every location has conventional fossil fuel resources. With the advances in renewable energy, wind and solar are close to competitive around the planet. As the Bush Administration pointed out in their National Energy Plan, renewables should be a top priority for local energy production when energy security is a concern. In 2001, when Bush revealed the National Energy Policy, renewables were not cost-competitive with conventional generation, but now conventional generation is barely cost competitive with renewables.[81]

AIR POLLUTION IS TOO EXPENSIVE

Likewise, the health consequences of air pollution from hydrocarbon energy sources are huge and have massive economic and human impacts. A plan to reduce global warming to 1.5 degrees centigrade could reduce health expenditures spent fighting conditions caused by air pollution by 5 percent of global GDP. In China, the effects of air pollution were linked to the premature deaths of 1.23 million people and a cost of 9–13 percent of total Chinese GDP in 2010.[82] For investors with a diversified portfolio, the greater economic growth is, the greater their personal wealth will grow. For investors with a portfolio focused on fast-growing economies, a cleaner, more prosperous world will benefit them greatly.

Overall, the costs of mitigating climate change and moving toward a zero-emissions electrical grid are immense and will require huge investments of capital and labor. The costs of inaction and business as usual are higher and will harm planetary development and slow, if not eliminate, economic growth. Cost is a substantial obstacle to making the grid

---

81 White House Archives, 2009, "Energy for America's Future," George Bush Whitehouse Archive, accessed December 10, 2019, https://georgewbush-whitehouse.archives.gov/infocus/energy/.

82 Grantham Research Institute on Climate Change and the Environment, 2018, "How Much Will It Cost to Cut Global Greenhouse Gas Emissions?" May 8, accessed December 10, 2019, http://www.lse.ac.uk/GranthamInstitute/faqs/how-much-will-it-cost-to-cut-global-greenhouse-gas-emissions/.

more flexible with storage and virtual power plants. In many cases, investing in a more flexible grid will provide a good return on investment. As long as regulation doesn't get in the way.

12

REGULATION

——

To call the Western grid Balkanized is an insult to Macedonia.
—JONATHON WEISGALL, BERKSHIRE HATHAWAY ENERGY

Excessive regulation could lead to slower adoption of energy storage and virtual power plants. Regulations can slow the deployment of energy storage and flexible production and demand in three primary ways: regulation shapes the structure of electrical markets, the time and effort to ensure compliance with regulation increases costs, which can decrease an asset's competitiveness, and the length of time it can take to complete additional surveys or studies can add up to project delays or longer project delivery cycles.

The different types of energy storage projects that are occurring also make the risk of regulatory issues larger: multiple technologies and differing project scales make sensible regulation challenging. The environmental reviews that may be appropriate for a utility-scale storage installation could add substantial and unnecessary costs to a much smaller commercial or residential project. Likewise, a large-scale molten salt thermal energy storage solution should probably have more comprehensive safety analysis requirements than a residential lithium-ion storage system.

Regulating many of these technologies requires expertise in the technology, business needs, and policy design. Local regulations usually end up imposing additional requirements on energy projects, and while not impossible, it is rare that smaller local governments have the foresight and staff to proactively update older regulations to accommodate cutting-edge energy projects. If regulations have to be modified before a project can commence, that will require a large amount of time, adding delays and lobbyist bills to a project's total cost.

PATCHWORK REGULATIONS

In the United States, these challenges are multiplied by fifty. Each state has its own regulations and unique requirements. This patchwork regulatory system can create unique challenges and opportunities for companies that are initiating energy projects but also reduces the optimal scale that most businesses in the sector can operate at. Each regulatory environment that a company does projects in requires them to maintain the staff and processes needed to ensure compliance with local requirements. The processes for installing identical assets could be radically different in terms of what the specific steps look like. This increases costs for a business doing projects in multiple regulatory areas.

In the United States, most electrical markets are structured through regulation, which can provide an uneven competitive landscape for storage projects. Likewise, the high speeds at which battery-based energy storage assets can charge, discharge, and switch from charging to discharging and vice versa are unique among other energy assets, and this makes pricing their services in a marketplace challenging. The Federal Energy Regulatory Commission (FERC) regulates energy distribution in the United States and has rolled out updated regulations to reflect the value that storage has:

"Electric storage resources have the ability both to charge and discharge electricity and can provide a variety of grid services to multiple entities (e.g., RTO/ISOs, transmission and distribution utilities) or in multiple markets. In addition, these resources are able to provide multiple services almost instantaneously and can switch from providing one service to another almost instantaneously. As such, electric storage resources may fit into one or more of the traditional asset functions of generation, transmission, and distribution. Enabling electric storage resources to provide multiple services (including both cost-based and market-based services) ensures that the full capabilities of these resources can be realized, thereby maximizing their efficiency and value for the system and to consumers."[83]

Getting the market structure correct is an important job for regulatory bodies. Bad market structure either underpays or overpays energy storage assets. Both of these are undesirable outcomes: underpayment for services does not fully incentivize the construction of new assets and paying too

83   Federal Energy Regulatory Commission, "Utilization of Electric Storage Resources for Multiple Services When Receiving Cost-Based Rate Recovery," 2019.

much increases costs to the ratepayers and end consumers of electricity. Good market structure and competitive pricing allow storage assets to be fairly compensated where they provide value and allows market signals to inform investment into future energy resources. Good regulation for market structure spurs investment and can lower costs overall, while bad regulation reduces investment, increases overall costs to most market participants, and can cause businesses to go bankrupt.

THE SILVER LINING: REGULATORY GOALS

While regulation is an obstacle that will have to be overcome to create a more flexible grid, in many countries and states, regulation is a driving force for adopting renewable energy. Numerous governments have decided that they must reach zero emissions by 2050, which requires almost all hydrocarbon electrical generation to be shut down. These regulatory requirements will give grid operators substantial incentives in most cases to move toward a grid that is flexible enough to meet these goals. Emissions goals in the United States are not as ambitious, but twenty-three states have passed laws or executive orders to substantially reduce emissions by 2050.

Overall, regulation is primarily a local risk to the speed of deployment of energy storage assets. For aggregated energy resources in the form of virtual power plants, a permissive regulatory environment that allows for entry into the electrical markets is required to do business.

13

TECHNOLOGY

———

*We are stuck with technology when what we really want is just
stuff that works.*

—DOUGLAS ADAMS, *THE SALMON OF DOUBT*

The coming revolution of a flexible power grid contains technological changes to how that energy is produced and consumed. The technological aspects of a flexible energy grid are critical variables that determine how quickly modern utilities and corporations will deploy flexible energy resources and how many flexible energy resources will be deployed compared to conventional assets. There is a nonzero possibility that the technological factors that are required for fast and near-total adoption of a flexible power grid simply do not occur. This chapter explores the likelihood and consequences of insufficient technological viability.

Two kinds of risks are useful to consider around energy technology: technology usage risks and technology development risks.

Most technologies come with known risks and dangers associated with their use or misuse. For example: using a heat source for cooking entails the risk that you may burn yourself or unintentionally create far more heat than desired and burn your house down. These risks are minimized by good technology design, safety measures, and adequate operator training. Having a properly engineered heat source that is robust, reliable, and predictable allows a well-trained operator to minimize the probability of accidents and harm when using the technology. Having safety measures and contingency plans in place allows incidents to be mitigated and resolved with minimal harm and cost: if an accidental fire occurs while cooking, fire extinguishers and an evacuation plan allow the fire to be contained or safely avoided. Likewise, having dedicated resources and people prepared to respond to emergencies—the fire department in this case—will help further minimize the cost and harm of rare technology-related incidents.

Automobiles are a great example of a commonplace energy-using technology that can massively improve quality of life and increase economic activity, while also killing tons of people. The World Health Organization estimates that 1.35 million people were killed in 2018 in vehicle-related accidents, up from 1.15 million in 2000. Vehicles—specifically the transportation sector—consume more than a third of global energy and were the eighth leading cause of death globally in 2015.[84] Vehicle operation is the most dangerous activity most

---

84 World Health Organization, "Global Status Report on Road Safety," 2018.

Americans ever perform (outside of behavioral activities—or the lack of behavioral activities in the case of heart disease and lifestyle illnesses). At the same time that vehicles are killing people, leaking oil, and filling the air with carbon, particulates, and smog, vehicles enable huge amounts of economic activity and improve the quality of life. The modern automobile is a technology that has massive benefits but also carries a lot of risks and creates danger.

The design, operator training, and safety measures of a modern automobile minimize the risks they create. Passenger automobiles are designed to be easy to operate: power steering and power breaking allow operators to easily steer and drive a car without having to exert large amounts of physical strength. Mirrors and windows are designed to assist operation on crowded roads. Many recently designed cars even include radar-based crash detection systems that will warn a driver if they are about to crash into something and automatically reduce speed to prevent the collision if no action is taken. In the event that a collision does occur, safety features like seat belts, airbags, and crumple zones reduce the impacts and likelihood of injury on vehicle passengers. Good design reduces the chance that vehicles will crash and minimizes injury to passengers when they do.

In most countries around the world, vehicle operators are required to have registration to legally operate a vehicle. These licenses typically require training in the safe operation of a vehicle and local norms, customs, and laws around vehicles. For some vehicles, multiple licenses are required. Large vehicles like buses and trucks require commercial drivers' licenses in many countries, which require additional training and certification. One of my brothers recently spent six weeks training to acquire a commercial driver's license in the United States. With training and experience, vehicles can be safely driven in numerous circumstances, and accidents can be dealt with as safely as possible.

With safety measures in place, a vehicle collision will cause less injury and damage. Barriers alongside roadways can prevent vehicles from leaving the roadway and crashing into pedestrians, structures, or other obstacles (at least on some roadways). Safe roadway design also creates buffer regions between vehicles, especially in higher-speed settings where an accident is likely to cause more damage. Having a median strip of grass between vehicles traveling in opposite directions reduces the likelihood of a head-on collision and gives a vehicle that leaves the roadway additional time to reduce speed to minimize the damage caused by a head-on collision or avoid it entirely by regaining control of the vehicle.

Likewise, good design, operator training, and safety measures reduce the risks of energy technology use. Every technology that produces, stores, or consumes energy carries some risk to its manufacture, usage, or disposal. Some of these risks are specific to groups of technologies, some are specific to individual instances of a particular technology, and some of these risks are inherent to all energy-related technologies.

Using engines and other prime movers to convert energy into motion carries a number of risks. With a well-designed engine maintained and operated correctly, accidents are rare. With safe system designs and emergency plans in place, damage caused by these accidents can be minimized. In most cases, the use and storage of the fuel source for an engine are more dangerous than the operation of the engine itself. Similarly, inappropriate operation or maintenance are the leading causes of accidents in most mature technological systems.

The energy source of most vehicles is energy dense for reasons of space: a denser fuel can store more energy in the same space. The specific energy—or energy per unit mass—of a fuel source is also important, especially for aviation and aerospace applications where weight is a critical factor. But in general, if a fuel source meets other criteria at a satisfactory cost, higher energy density and specific energy is ideal. This energy density causes issues, though, because the risk of accidents becoming harmful increases as the energy involved rises. A battery or fuel tank that catches on fire cannot release more energy than it contains. For electric vehicles that contain increasingly larger and more energy-dense batteries, this risk becomes particularly large.

Tesla Motors has experienced issues with the battery packs in its cars for as long as it has made cars. This is because of two factors: the first reason is that severe automobile crashes that cause massive structural damage are difficult to design for and usually cause damage to the battery packs. The second reason is that lithium-ion battery packs are challenging to design and manufacture at large scales.

The cylindrical 18650 lithium-ion batteries that Tesla uses are generally designed to be puncture-proof by having a strong steel casing. This casing adds weight but helps with thermal management and reduces the risk of accidental short circuits.

If the anode and cathode of a lithium-ion battery are directly connected, the battery short circuits, which causes the battery to heat up. For a low-density battery, a short circuit like this is unlikely to cause enough heat to cause a fire. For a lithium-ion battery, rapid discharges—like those caused by a short circuit—can cause thermal runaway, or in layman's terms: an explosion.

Batteries have internal resistance. Modern batteries are designed to minimize internal resistance, but it is impossible to eliminate in practice. Internal resistance inside a battery means that heating will occur when the battery is used. Resistance increases with temperature inside of batteries, so the resistance that is causing heating will increase the hotter a battery gets. This means that at high discharge rates, a battery without sufficient cooling will get hotter and hotter. This internal resistance also causes internal heating proportional to the rate of discharge. In an electrical circuit where Ohm's law applies, voltage is equal to current times resistance: $V = IR$. This means that a battery that is being used heavily will either see a decrease in voltage or current as internal resistance rises. For a lead-acid battery, thermal runaway almost never occurs because the voltage drops quickly as temperature increases.

For lithium-ion batteries, however, due to the chemistry involved, heating a lithium-ion battery can cause the voltage to increase slightly due to increased chemical activity, which allows the battery to deliver more current. This increase in voltage offsets the increased internal resistance that occurs at higher temperatures. So unlike a lead-acid or nickel-cadmium battery, a lithium-ion battery discharging at excessively high current rates can continue discharging without as large a voltage drop, leaving more power to be dissipated internally. This means that a lithium-ion battery without adequate cooling that is being discharged at high rates or short-circuited can overheat. Most lithium-ion batteries use flammable electrolytes that can catch fire at high temperatures. A rapid increase in temperature can cause the pressure of this electrolyte to increase inside the metal cell casing, leading to the cell's safety valve venting the hot, flammable electrolyte gases. If the temperature has gotten hot enough, these vented gases will catch fire, leading to even higher temperatures and the cell will spew fire and hot debris. A catastrophic failure of one cell can cascade to nearby cells, leading to catastrophic runaway thermal events inside of an entire battery pack.

A kilogram of TNT has an energy content of approximately 1.162 kWh. This means that an 85 kWh battery contains the equivalent energy of more than 70 kilograms of TNT. While lithium-ion batteries are far safer to handle than explosives, they also contain large amounts of energy that can be dangerous. Good manufacturing techniques for individual cells and battery packs reduce the risk of fire.

Unless a piece of metal road debris gets kicked up by the tires and punctures an electric vehicle's battery pack, causing the battery pack to catch fire.

On November 6, 2013, a Tesla Model S struck a metal trailer towing hitch at 70 mph, which punctured the battery through a quarter-inch thick protective aluminum plate. The car detected the damage to the vehicle and warned the driver to pull over. The driver pulled over and exited the vehicle. A few minutes later, about five minutes in total after the battery pack was punctured, the battery pack caught fire and destroyed the front of the vehicle. The passenger compartment was unharmed by the fire, and the driver was later able to retrieve papers from the glove compartment.[85]

A few weeks prior to the November 6 crash, another Tesla Model S caught fire. This vehicle struck a concrete wall at 110 mph, knocking down fifteen feet of wall and impacting a large tree. This collision tore off the front wheel and smashed the front section of the vehicle. Again, the car warned the driver to exit the vehicle and then caught fire a few minutes later. The driver walked away with only minor injuries from a 110 mph crash, and the battery fire was extinguished by the fire department.

In response to these fires, Tesla added additional armor plating to the underside of the Model S, including a titanium plate. Elon Musk wrote in a blog post published in 2014 that the added titanium shield could destroy or deflect most road debris and that the previous design already provided substantial safety:

"As the empirical evidence suggests, the underbody shields are not needed for a high level of safety. However, there is significant value to minimizing owner inconvenience in the event of an impact and addressing any lingering public misperception about electric vehicle safety. With a track record of zero deaths

---

85   Jay Cole, "Third Tesla Model S Fire: The Owner's Story," InsideEVs, November 9, 2013, https://insideevs.com/news/319265/third-tesla-model-el-s-fire-the-owners-story

*or serious, permanent injuries since our vehicles went into
production six years ago, there is no safer car on the road than
a Tesla. The addition of the underbody shields simply takes
it a step further.*"[86]

While Tesla builds vehicles with excellent safety features,
operator misuse continues to cause accidents. Crash-test
ratings and Tesla-sponsored research confirm that in most
cases, including extreme crashes, the vehicles are at least as
safe if not far safer than gasoline-powered vehicles. These
safe vehicles can still cause death and injury, and the battery
design and safety features can't prevent every injury when
the car is literally driven into walls or off cliffs. There have
been incidents where Model S vehicles have been involved in
high-speed crashes that ended in fatal fires due to damage to
the battery pack.[87] Overall, Tesla vehicles are safe—if I had
to pick a vehicle to drive into a concrete wall at high speed,
a Tesla vehicle would be at the top of the list—but there are
unique technological risks and hazards that apply to electric
vehicles that rely on lithium-ion batteries. These risks may
be less than the similar risks of fire from collisions involving
gasoline-powered vehicles, but they cannot be ignored.

Electric vehicle batteries catching fire after extreme crashes
is unsurprising. What is more surprising is when the battery
catches fire during charging. This is a risk with all batteries,

---

86   Elon Musk, "Tesla Adds Titanium Underbody Shield and Aluminum
     Deflector Plates to Model S," Tesla, Inc., September 25, 2014, https://
     www.tesla.com/blog/tesla-adds-titanium-underbody-shield-and-alu-
     minum-deflector-plates-model-s.

87   Sanjana Shivdas, "Tesla Fires Since 2013 Listed," Autoblog, May 11,
     2018, https://www.autoblog.com/2018/05/11/a-list-of-tesla-car-fires-
     since-2013/.

as lead-acid batteries get hot and can vent flammable hydrogen gas while charging. With lithium-ion batteries, the charge cycle also creates heat internally, which can lead to catastrophic thermal runaway in situations with insufficient cooling. Large lithium-ion battery packs contain active cooling solutions that employ forced air or pumped liquid cooling and will shut off parts of the battery if they get too hot, even shutting down completely if they get too hot. High-speed charging is currently limited by temperature and battery longevity. Tesla appears to have the battery longevity optimized fairly well, but the supercharging is limited by how hot the batteries can safely get.

On June 1, a Tesla caught fire while using a Tesla Supercharger station in Belgium and was destroyed in the flames. After the emergency responders extinguished the fire, the fire department submerged the vehicle in water overnight to ensure that the battery did not reignite.[88] This technique of submerging battery fires in water to ensure no reignition occurs is an example of improving emergency response plans. A previous fire had occurred in the United States where a Model X Tesla was damaged in a fire (possibly started while it was charging) and then reignited after being towed to a local garage.

These charging incidents are unfortunate and surprising, but what is more surprising is the battery fires that occur spontaneously. There have been several documented cases of Tesla vehicles spontaneously catching fire while parked.

---

88 Jan Alberts, "Brandende Tesla Moet Nachtje in Bad Om Vlammen Te Doven," HLN (DPG Media, June 2, 2019), https://www.hln.be/in-de-buurt/antwerpen/brandende-tesla-moet-nachtje-in-bad-om-vlam-men-te-doven~a112edf9.

They have apparently not been plugged in or involved with a collision in any way. Tesla pushed out a software update to the thermal management system for several car models after a Model S caught fire while parked and off in Hong Kong in early May of 2019.[89] There were two other incidents of Tesla vehicles catching fire without any obvious cause in April and May of 2019. Tesla is investigating these incidents and has not commented on the cause.

One potential cause of these fires is defects in the battery pack. A Tesla 85 KWh battery can contain more than 7,100 individual lithium-ion battery cells. Tesla's Gigafactory in Reno, Nevada, has produced over 500 million lithium-ion cells in the three years since it opened in 2016 and has ambitious goals to produce billions of battery cells annually when completed.[90] While Tesla's processes are good and they produce high-quality battery cells, battery packs, and battery management systems, at manufacturing scales like that with electrochemical devices as complicated as lithium-ion batteries, it is not unlikely that a battery cell could have failed due to a manufacturing defect in a way that caused an internal short circuit. If this failing cell was missed by the battery management system, it could have begun overheating before going into thermal runaway and lighting the battery pack on fire. The thermal management system should have prevented

---

89   Jonathon Klein, "Parked Teslas Keep Catching on Fire Randomly, and There's No Recall In Sight," The Drive, June 18, 2019, https://www. thedrive.com/news/28420/parked-teslas-keep-catching-on-fire-randomly-and-theres-no-recall-in-sight.

90   Fred Lambert, "Tesla Gigafactory 1 Has Already Produced over Half a Billion Battery Cells," Electrek, January 14, 2019, https://electrek. co/2019/01/12/tesla-gigafactory-1-produced-half-billion-battery-cells/.

a single cell failure from cascading to the rest of the battery, but the cars still managed to catch on fire.

There are substantial risks to the use of energy storage technologies, but the risks are manageable and should not overshadow the benefits

TECHNOLOGY DEVELOPMENT RISKS

The second kind of technology risk is the risk of technological development. New technologies that are being developed usually are rough around the edges and are harder, more dangerous, and more expensive to use than contemporary technologies. As a technology is developed further, it usually becomes safer, easier to use, and cheaper. The risk of developing new technology or improving current technology is that these improvements in safety, operation, and cost do not occur, or do not occur as fast or as affordably as expected.

Tesla's Prospectus before its Initial Public Offering of stock in 2010 listed technological development risks as a known risk that could cause them to fail. They even included comments detailing the risks their business and customers faced from using lithium-ion batteries:

"We have designed our battery pack to passively contain any single cell's release of energy without spreading to neighboring cells and we are not aware of any such incident in our customers' vehicles. We have tested the batteries and subjected them to damaging treatments such as baking, overcharging, crushing, or puncturing to assess our battery pack's response to deliberate and sometimes destructive abuse. However, we

have delivered only a limited number of Tesla Roadsters to customers and have limited field experience with our vehicles. Accordingly, there can be no assurance that a field failure of our battery packs will not occur, which could damage the vehicle or lead to personal injury or death and may subject us to lawsuits."[91]

With renewable energy sources, especially wind and solar, the technologies are far enough along in development that they are now relatively low risk compared to where they were just a few years ago. Most types of energy storage are still maturing. Much of the maturation of energy storage is due to increases in scale: building more energy storage allows economies of scale to bring the cost down, and large volumes increase the value of further research and development.

There are still risks in the development of energy storage and more flexible consumption, but at this point, the largest risks are that the costs don't decrease as fast as expected. There are no questions that energy storage works and that storage and aggregated demand response are functional technologies that deliver substantial economic and environmental benefits. The real question is are they cost-competitive with conventional energy resources? There is a chance that the regular operational costs and dangers are not improved or are improved insufficiently by future technological development. Overall, this risk is low given the globally recognized costs and risks of conventional energy assets that are not currently accounted for.

---

91   US Security and Exchange Commission "Tesla Motors, Inc. Form S-1 Registration Statement," 2010, accessed December 10, 2019.

Overall, all the obstacles to a more flexible grid are surmountable and are unlikely to do more than slow the transition to a more reliable, sustainable, and affordable grid. So what does the future of the electrical grid look like?

14

2030: THE HYBRID GRID

…We know that generating more clean energy, using less dirty energy, and wasting less energy overall can be good for business and consumers. And it's also good for the world that we leave for our children.

—BARACK OBAMA, REMARKS BY THE PRESIDENT ON AMERICAN ENERGY

What will the US electrical grid look like in 2030?

The electrical grid is going to move toward a hybrid grid. The start of this transition has been visible for the last few years, and the trends driving this transition are going to accelerate. The two dimensions of the transition to a hybrid grid are the shift from conventional hydrocarbon generation to renewable energy and the shift from centralized generation to distributed energy resources.[92] The three primary driving factors behind these shifts are the falling costs of renewable

---

92   ISO New England, "The Rapid Transformation of New England's Power System and Implications for Wholesale Electricity Markets," Boston Economic Club, 2019.

generation, the falling costs of distributed energy resources, and the desire to reduce carbon emissions and have a sustainable grid.

HYDROCARBON TO RENEWABLE

Hydrocarbon energy sources for electrical generation are likely to decline by 2030. The total amount of electricity consumed in the US is likely to rise slowly by 2030, with much of this growth coming from electric vehicles. By 2030, almost the entirety of hydrocarbon electrical generation will be natural gas due to the lower cost of natural gas.

To minimize planetary warming, carbon emissions will need to be decreasing substantially by 2030. Almost half the states in the US have mandatory or aspirational goals that commit them to reduce emissions by 2050.[93] Many of these commitments are to reduce emissions to below 1990 or 2005 levels by 2025 or 2030. To reduce greenhouse gas emissions and meet these targets, most sectors of the economy will have to become more efficient and substitute emitting energy sources for carbon-free sources. The most obvious substitutions are wind and solar for coal and gas. Gas emits less per kWh than coal, and so will still be a substantial part of the grid's energy mix in 2030.

Coal generation will decline substantially due to market forces and plant retirements. It is likely that regulatory action will occur that will be the nail in coal's coffin either

---

93　"US State Greenhouse Gas Emissions Targets," Center for Climate and Energy Solutions, July 8, 2019, https://www.c2es.org/document/greenhouse-gas-emissions-targets/.

in the form of a carbon tax or more stringent air pollution requirements. By 2030, coal will provide less than 20 percent of electricity and could provide less than 10 percent if the cost of gas stays low and renewables become even cheaper. A national carbon tax could further accelerate this shift by increasing costs for hydrocarbon generation.

Solar and wind will increase its market share. If the solar investment tax credits are phased out at the end of 2024 as currently scheduled, solar installation will slow slightly in the latter half of the decade.[94] It is likely that solar deployment will speed up and exceed many projections as costs continue to fall. Wind will also continue to increase capacity as larger turbines are deployed and more projects are built. In many regions, the majority of new generation built will be wind and solar.

THE DECENTRALIZING GRID

By 2030, a large portion of total electrical capacity and generation will come from distributed energy resources. In some regions, small scale solar could account for the majority of solar capacity additions. The majority of electricity is still going to come from centralized power stations, but in most regions, enough energy will come from distributed sources that grid operators will have to make substantial investments in grid stability.

---

94 "Annual Energy Outlook 2019" (US Energy Information Administration—EIA, January 24, 2019), https://www.eia.gov/outlooks/aeo/.

The grid will need to be more flexible to accommodate decentralization.

Regional differences will be more visible in ten years: some states will have embraced the energy transition willingly and gotten ahead of the stresses caused by the growing integration of renewable resources; others will be caught in a bind between well-intentioned regulation requiring more low-carbon energy and the constraints of path dependency and market realities. Utilities and grid operators that embrace the energy transition wisely will be able to deliver better service more reliably at a potentially lower price. Energy companies that choose to be ignorant of the evolving energy landscape will find themselves eviscerated by the winds of change. Also solar-plus-storage.

The only scenario that can stop the energy transition is global conflict, which I hope is unlikely.

15

CONCLUSION

———

*We live in a sea of electricity. Our grid, for now, is the means
we use to bring this electricity home. It warms and nourishes
us. It makes life in extreme environments like Fargo and Phoe-
nix livable, even comfortable. Despite being surrounded by
this abundance of power, if we cannot make the means to this
electricity more reliably our own, we too could die of 'thirst.' It
does not matter how much water is in the sea, or how much
electricity we generate, if that water is not drinkable and that
electricity is not delivered.*

—GRETCHEN BAKKE, *THE GRID*

The electrical grid of the future will contain energy storage
and flexible energy assets, many of which are virtual power
plants aggregated out of electric vehicles and behind-the-
meter storage and appliances. I have addressed many of the
ways that storage and grid flexibility increase the stability
of the grid while reducing costs and carbon emissions and
increasing the dispatch rate for renewable energy. The costs
of storage are widely expected to continue dropping in the
future, while the operating costs for hydrocarbon-based

power plants are expected to rise, leading to further widespread adoption of low-carbon energy production and storage for both bulk storage and intermittent asset firming.

There are three core takeaways that I want to make explicit:

- Within a few years, energy storage will be present in almost every electric grid around the planet. The amount of storage deployed will depend on how fast the costs drop and how expensive current frequency control services are.
- Virtual power plants—aggregated groups of smaller energy resources like electric vehicles and home energy storage—will become an increasingly important part of integrating intermittent renewable generation with conventional power assets over the next decade. By 2030, many electrical markets with both high renewable penetration and high storage or electric vehicle market penetration will utilize some form of virtual power plant to reduce costs.
- We can take the future of energy into our own hands at the individual, local, regional, and national levels. It is possible to generate all the electricity we need in most regions from renewable energy alone, but the grid needs to be more flexible to accommodate this.

We live in interesting times that are full of opportunities and challenges. Increasing the flexibility of the grid using energy storage and virtual power plants will make our civilization more resilient in the face of a changing climate and social and political turmoil and allow us to move toward a more sustainable presence on this pale blue dot we all call home.

WORKS CITED

ABC News. 2018. "How Australia Survived Its Second Hottest Sumer Without Load-Shedding Blackouts." May 23. Accessed December 10, 2019. https://www.abc.net.au/news/2018-05-23/no-load-shedding-over-hot-summer/9792802.

Apple. 2019. "Battery Service and Recycling." Accessed December 10, 2019. https://www.apple.com/batteries/service-and-recycling/.

Aurecon. 2019. "Hornsdale Power Reserve Year 1 Technical and Market Impact Case Study." Aurecon.

Australian Energy Market Operator. 2018. Preliminary Report—Queensland and South Australia System Seperation on 25 August 2018. AEMO.

Australian Financial Review. 2019. "AEMO: Generators Must Do Better When Grid Wobbles." January 10. Accessed December 10, 2019. https://www.afr.com/politics/aemo-generators-must-do-better-when-grid-wobbles-20190109-h19vu9.

Australian Renewable Energy Agency. 2019. "AGL Virtual Power
    Plant." October 25. Accessed December 10, 2019. https://
    arena.gov.au/projects/agl-virtual-power-plant/.

Autoblog. 2018. "A List of Tesla Car Fires Since 2013." May
    11. Accessed December 10, 2019. https://www.autoblog.
    com/2018/05/11/a-list-of-tesla-car-fires-since-2013/.

Bloomberg. 2019. "Battery Reality: There's Nothing Better Than
    Lithium-Ion Coming Soon." April 3. Accessed December 10,
    2019. https://www.bloomberg.com/news/articles/2019-04-03/
    battery-reality-there-s-nothing-better-than-lithium-ion-
    coming-soon.

California Independent System Operator. 2016. *What the Duck
    Curve Tells Us about Managing a Green Grid.* Folsom: CAISO.

Carter, Jimmy. 1980. "January 23, 1980: State of the Union
    Address." 1 23. Accessed December 9, 2019. https://
    millercenter.org/the-presidency/presidential-speeches/
    january-23-1980-state-union-address.

Center for Climate and Energy Solutions. 2019. "US State
    Greenhouse Gas Emissions Targets." July. Accessed
    December 10, 2019. https://www.c2es.org/document/
    greenhouse-gas-emissions-targets/.

Center for Climate and Security. 2017. "The Climate Factor
    in Syrian Instability." September 8. Accessed December
    10, 2019. https://climateandsecurity.org/2017/09/08/the-
    climate-factor-in-syrian-instability-a-conversation-worth-
    continuing/.

Center for Global Development. 2017. "The Electricity Situation in Ghana: Challenges and Opportunities." Washington, DC: Center for Global Development.

Center for Sustainable Systems Univertsity of Michigan. 2019. US Energy Storage Factsheet. Accessed December 10, 2019. http://css.umich.edu/factsheets/us-grid-energy-storage-factsheet.

Cleantechnica. 2019. "Electric Vehicle To Grid Technology Gears Up for the Mass Market." January 26. Accessed December 10, 2019. https://cleantechnica.com/2019/01/26/electric-vehicle-to-grid-technology-gears-up-for-the-mass-market-cleantechnica-interview/.

Climate KIC. 2018. "No More Excuses: Financing 1.5C." October 11. Accessed December 10, 2019. https://www.climate-kic.org/news/no-more-excuses-financing-1-5c/.

Climate Vulnurable Forum. 2016. "Pursuing the 1.5C Limit: Benefits & Opportunities." *Low Carbon Monitor.*

Coindesk. 2019. "What Is Blockchain Technology?" September 2019. Accessed December 10, 2019. https://www.coindesk.com/information/what-is-the-difference-between-open-and-permissioned-blockchains.

Con Edison. 2017. REV Demonstation Project: Clean Virtual Power PLant 2016 Q4 Quarterly Progress Report. Con Edison.

Corean, Michael J. 2016. *Quartz.* May 10. Accessed 2019. https://qz.com/680661/germany-had-so-much-renewable-energy-on-sunday-that-it-had-to-pay-people-to-use-electricity/.

Degroot, Dagomar. 2017. "Tipping Points." 4 7. Accessed December 9, 2019. https://www.climatetippingpoints.com/places/washington-dc-future-climate-change.

Degroot, Dagomeer. 2018. *The Frigid Golden Age.* Cambridge University Press.

DPG Media. 02019. "Brandende Tesla Moet Nachtje in Bad Om Vlammen Te Doven." June 2. Accessed December 10, 2019. https://www.hln.be/in-de-buurt/antwerpen/brandende-tesla-moet-nachtje-in-bad-om-vlammen-te-doven~a112edf9/.

Electrek. 2019. "Tesla Gigafactory 1 Has Already Produced Over Half a Billion Battery Cells." January 12. Accessed December 10, 2019. https://electrek.co/2019/01/12/tesla-gigafactory-1-produced-half-billion-battery-cells/.

Electric Transmission Texas. 2010. "Presidio NAS Batteery Project Facts at a Glance." *ETTexas.com.* 5 4. Accessed December 10, 2019. http://www.ettexas.com/Content/documents/NaSBatteryOverview.pdf.

Energy Storage News. 2015. "Failed Battery at Hawaii Solar Farm Part of Learning Process Says Analyst." January 21. Accessed December 10, 2019. https://www.energy-storage.news/news/accelerated-capacity-fade-of-battery-at-hawaii-solar-farm-part-of-learning.

—. 2019. "UAE Integrates 648 MWh of Sodium Sulfur Batteries in One Swoop." January 28. Accessed December 10, 2019. https://www.energy-storage.news/news/uae-integrates-648mwh-of-sodium-sulfur-batteries-in-one-swoop.

Federal Energy Regulatory Commission. 2019. "Utilization of Electric Storage Resources for Multiple Services When Receiving Cost-Based Rate Recovery." Washington, DC: FERC.

Fleetcarma. 2019. "Smart Charge New York." Accessed December 10, 2019. https://www.fleetcarma.com/smartchargenewyork/.

Golden Valley Electric Association. n.d. "Battery Energy Storage System." Accessed December 10, 2019. https://www.gvea.com/energy/bess.

Grahm, Karen. 2018. "Tesla's Big Battery in Australia Has Defied All Expectations." October 4. Accessed December 10, 2019. http://www.digitaljournal.com/tech-and-science/technology/tesla-s-big-battery-in-australia-has-defied-all-expectations/article/533773.

Grantham Research Institute on Climate Change and the Environment. 2018. "How Much Will It Cost to Cut Global Greenhouse Gas Emissions?" May 8. Accessed December 10, 2019. http://www.lse.ac.uk/GranthamInstitute/faqs/how-much-will-it-cost-to-cut-global-greenhouse-gas-emissions/.

Green Mountain Power. 2017. "GMP Launches New Comprehensive Energy Home Solution from Tesla to Lower Costs for Custoemrs." May 12. Accessed December 10, 2019.

https://greenmountainpower.com/news/gmp-launches-new-comprehensive-energy-home-solution-tesla-lower-costs-customers/.

Green Tech Media. 2018. "EMotorWerks Is Using Its Network of 10,000 EV Chargers to Bid into Wholesale Markets." September 25. Accessed 12 10, 2019. https://www.greentechmedia.com/articles/read/emotorwerks-wholesale-markets-ev-charger-network#gs.l4r5rj.

—. 2018. "Why PV Costs Have Fallen So Far—and Will Fall Further." December 14. Accessed December 9, 2019. https://www.greentechmedia.com/articles/read/why-pv-costs-have-fallen-so-far-and-will-fall-further.

Hal Harvey, Robbie Orvis, Jeffrey Rissman. 2018. *Designing Climate Solutions.* Island Press/Center for Resource Economics.

Hanley, Steve. 2017. "Vehicle to Grid Plan Pays Off for Electric Car Drivers in Europe." August 18. Accessed December 10, 2019. https://enrg.io/vehicle-grid-plan-pays-off-electric-car-drivers-europe/.

Inside EVs. 2013. "Third Tesla Model S Fire: the Owner's Story." November 09. Accessed December 10, 2019. https://insideevs.com/news/319265/third-tesla-model-s-fire-the-owners-story/.

ISO New England. 2019. "Final 2019 PV Forecast." Holyoke, MA: ISO New England.

ISO New England. 2019. *The Rapid Transformation of New England's Power System and Implications for Wholesale Electricity Markets.* Boston, MA: Boston Economic Club.

Lawrence Livermore National Laboratory. "National Ignition Facility and Photon Science." Accessed December 10, 2019. https://lasers.llnl.gov/about/how-nif-works/beamline/power-conditioning.

Lazard. 2016. *Levelized Cost of Energy Analysis Version 10.* Lazard.

—. 2018. "Levelized Cost of Energy and Levelized Cost of Storage 2018." November 8. Accessed December 10, 2019. https://www.lazard.com/perspective/levelized-cost-of-energy-and-levelized-cost-of-storage-2018/.

Lazard. 2018. *Levelized Cost of Storage Version 4.0.* Lazard. https://www.lazard.com/media/450774/lazards-levelized-cost-of-storage-version-40-vfinal.pdf.

Liu, W., Xu, Z., & Yang, T. 2018. "Health Effects of Air Pollution in China." *International Journal of Environmental Research and Public Health*, 1471.

Live, Navy. 2018. "Keeping Our Sights on Target: A Strategic Vision for Energy Security." 2 2. Accessed December 9, 2019. https://navylive.dodlive.mil/2018/02/02/keeping-our-sights-on-target-a-strategic-vision-for-energy-security/.

McKinsey. 2016. "The New Economics of Energy Storage." August. Accessed December 10, 2019. https://www.mckinsey.

com/business-functions/sustainability/our-insights/the-new-economics-of-energy-storage.

National Renewable Energy Laboratory. 2008. *Production Cost Modeling for High Levels of Photovoltaics Penetration.* Midwest Research Institute.

Navy, US. 2009. "US Navy Energy, Environment, and Climate Change." Accessed December 9, 2019. https://navysustainability.dodlive.mil/energy/.

Nef, John U. 1977. "An Early Energy Crisis and Its Consequences." *Scientific American,* 140–151.

Neoen. 2019. "Hornsdale Power Reserve." Accessed December 10, 2019. https://hornsdalepowerreserve.com.au/.

News Corp Australia. 2016. "Man Makes Mini Battery Power Station In His Home After Buying Six Tesla Powerwalls." September 14. Accessed December 10, 2019. https://www.news.com.au/technology/innovation/inventions/man-makes-mini-battery-power-station-in-his-home-after-buying-six-tesla-powerwalls/news-story/4a09a5ed7a87515a27 6af68b6a1296c6.

Nova, Joanne. 2019. "Report on Aug 25 Blackouts Shows How Fragile Our Grid Is." January 11. Accessed December 10, 2019. http://joannenova.com.au/2019/01/report-on-aug-25-blackouts-shows-how-fragile-our-grid-is-and-the-real-cost-of-cheap-solar-panels/.

Power Magazine. 2015. "Leveraging Fuel Flexibility for Coal Power Plant Survival." 9 1. Accessed December 9, 2019. https://www.powermag.com/leveraging-fuel-flexibility-for-coal-power-plant-survival/.

RAND Corporation. 2015. *Cost of Selected Policies to Address Air Pollution in China.* Santa Monica: RAND Corporation. https://www.rand.org/content/dam/rand/pubs/research_reports/RR800/RR861/RAND_RR861.pdf.

Rocky Mountain Institute. 2018. *The Economics of Clean Energy Portfolios.* Rocky Mountain Institute.

Royal Swedish Acedemy of Sciences. 2019. *Press Release: The Nobel Prize in Chemistry 2019.* October 9. Accessed December 10, 2019. https://www.nobelprize.org/prizes/chemistry/2019/press-release/.

San Antonio Business Journal. 2019. "Report Shows Texas 2nd in Nation for Clean Energy Jobs." March 14. Accessed December 10, 2019. https://www.bizjournals.com/sanantonio/news/2019/03/14/report-shows-texas-2nd-in-nation-for-clean-energy.html.

Science Policy Circle. 2019. "The 'Peakers': The Role of Peaking Power Plants and Their Relevance Today." Accessed December 10, 2019. https://www.sciencepolicycircle.org/38-the-peakers-the-role-of-peaking-power-plants-and-their-relevance-today.

SF Gate. 2003. "State of Transition/End of the Davis Era." 11 12. Accessed December 9, 2019. https://www.sfgate.com/politics/

article/STATE-OF-TRANSITION-End-of-the-Davis-era-2549307.php.

Solar Magazine. 2018. "Chile's 24x7 Concentrating Solar Power Plus Storage Project Is Back on Track." June 4. Accessed December 10, 2019. https://solarmagazine.com/chiles-24x7-concentrating-solar-power-plus-storage-project-is-back-on-track/.

Tennessee Valley Authority. n.d. "The TVA Act." Accessed December 9, 2019. https://www.tva.gov/About-TVA/Our-History/The-TVA-Act.

Tesla Motors, Inc. 2010. "Form S-1 Registration Statement." Washington, DC: US Security and Exchange Commission.

Tesla. 2014. "Tesla Adds Titanium Underbody Shield and Aluminium Deflector Plates to Model S." March 28. Accessed December 10, 2019. https://www.tesla.com/blog/tesla-adds-titanium-underbody-shield-and-aluminum-deflector-plates-model-s.

The Associated Press. 2019. "Tankers Struck Near Strait of Hormuz." 6 13. Accessed December 9, 2019. https://apnews.com/d67714ab8ac344a3b3af19cca1c20192.

The Drive. 2019. "Parked Teslas Keep Catching on Fire Randomly." June 18. Accessed December 10, 2019. https://www.thedrive.com/news/28420/parked-teslas-keep-catching-on-fire-randomly-and-theres-no-recall-in-sight.

The Driven. 2019. "Electric Cars Can Smooth Grid and Reduce Energy Prices." April 9. Accessed December 10, 2019. https://thedriven.io/2019/04/09/electric-cars-can-smooth-grid-and-reduce-energy-prices-report-says/.

The World Bank. 2019. "World Bank Open Data." Accessed December 9, 2019. https://data.worldbank.org/.

US Department of Energy. 2014. "The History of The Electric Car." September 15. Accessed December 9, 2019. https://www.energy.gov/articles/history-electric-car.

US Energy Information Administration. 2019. *Annual Energy Outlook 2019.* Washington, DC: US Energy Information Administration.

—. 2019. "Form EIA-860 Detailed Data." September 3. Accessed December 10, 2019. https://www.eia.gov/electricity/data/eia860/.

—. 2019. "Monthly Energy Review." November 25. Accessed December 9, 2019. https://www.eia.gov/totalenergy/data/monthly/index.php#environment.

—. 2018. "Today In Energy." 8 27. Accessed December 9, 2019. https://www.eia.gov/todayinenergy/detail.php?id=36952.

—. 2019. "Today in Energy: The Strait of Hormuz is the World's Most Important Oil Transit Chokepoint." 6 20. Accessed December 9, 2019. https://www.eia.gov/todayinenergy/detail.php?id=39932.

—. 2019. "Wholesale Electricity and Natural Gas Market Data." December 5. Accessed December 10, 2019. https://www.eia.gov/electricity/wholesale/.

US Government Accountability Office. 2017. "Information on Potential Ecnomic Effects Could Help Guide Federal Efforts to Reduce Fiscal Exposure." October 24. Accessed December 10, 2019. https://www.gao.gov/products/GAO-17-720.

Ulieru, Dr. Mihaela, interview by William Angel. 2019. Primary Interview for Research on Virtual Power, February 22, 2019.

UN Economic and Social Council. 2016. *Progress Towards the Sustainable Development Goals.* Report of the Secretary-General, UN Economic and Social Council.

Universal Ecological Fund. 2017. "The Economic Case for Climate Action in the United States." September. Accessed December 10, 2019. https://feu-us.org/case-for-climate-action-us/.

University of Sourthern California. 2015. "Fukushima Disaster Was Preventable." September 21. Accessed December 10, 2019. https://news.usc.edu/86362/fukushima-disaster-was-preventable-new-study-finds/.

Utility Dive. 2018. "EMotorWerks Provides CAISO with 30 MW of DR Through Smart EV charging." September 12. Accessed December 10, 2019. https://www.utilitydive.com/news/emotorwerks-provides-caiso-with-30-mw-of-dr-through-smart-ev-charging/532110/.

—. 2014. "Pepco Enrolls Half of Eligible Comverge Demand Response Customers." December 23. Accessed December 10, 2019. https://www.utilitydive.com/news/pepco-enrolls-half-of-eligible-comverge-demand-response-customers/346805/.

—. 2017. "Software Upgrade to Old Sodium Battery Marks Shift in AEP's Storage Strategy." May 9. Accessed December 10, 2019. https://www.utilitydive.com/news/software-upgrade-to-old-sodium-battery-marks-shift-in-aeps-storage-strateg/442223/.

Welton, Shelley. 2018. "Grasping for Energy Democracy." *Michigan Law Review.*

White House Archives. 2009. "Energy For America's Future George Bush White House Archive." Accessed December 10, 2019. https://georgewbush-whitehouse.archives.gov/infocus/energy/.

Wirfs-Brock, Jordan. 2014. "IE Questions: Why Is California Trying to Behead the Duck." October. Accessed December 9, 2019. http://insideenergy.org/2014/10/02/ie-questions-why-is-california-trying-to-behead-the-duck/.

World Health Organization. 2018. "Global Status Report on Road Safety 2018." WHO.

World Sailing Speed Record Council. 2019. "24-Hour Distance Records." Accessed December 9, 2019. https://www.sailspeedrecords.com/24-hour-distance.

Yergin, Daniel. *The Quest: Energy, Security and the Remaking of the Modern World.* London: Penguin, 2012.

Yergin, Daniel. *The Prize: the Epic Quest for Oil, Money & Power.* London: Simon & Schuster, 2012.